Hebridean Princess

IN PICTURES

As the 25th cruising season of *Hebridean Princess* approaches, it gives me great pleasure to recommend this splendid photographic documentary by Bryan Kennedy, of her voyages since conversion from a Caledonian MacBrayne ferry to the luxurious, five star vessel she is today.

Hebridean Princess has rekindled the golden age of cruising, carrying just 50 guests with a crew of 38 to cruise the waters of Scotland's west coast and Western Isles with occasional forays to the Northern Isles of Orkney and Shetland, Norway, France, Ireland and the south coast of England.

In January 2012 Hebridean Island Cruises was granted a Royal Warrant by Her Majesty the Queen in recognition of the holidays that she and other members of the Royal Family have enjoyed on *Hebridean Princess* - the only cruise ship to have been given such an accolade.

This prestigious award is a tribute to the unprecedented quality of luxury and personal service aboard and ashore and the crews who deliver it.

I trust you will enjoy this historical chronicle of *Hebridean Princess* and her destinations.

Lord Sterling
Chairman, Hebridean Island Cruises

3

3   At the gleaming brass helm of the *Hebridean Princess*.

4   *The Columba* alongside at Colonsay on 12th June, 1987.
     (photo courtesy of Anthony Williams)

5   "By Appointment" - The Royal Arms sits proudly aboard the ship. Awarded at the beginning of 2012 to All Leisure Holidays, owners of the *Hebridean Princess*, in recognition of services supplied for at least five years to HM The Queen, HRH the Duke of Edinburgh or HRH the Prince of Wales, it is the first time a Royal Warrant has been awarded to a shipping company.

6   Reborn as the *Hebridean Princess* leaving Great Yarmouth in 1989.
     (photo courtesy of Jim Pottinger)

1-2 Completely self-sufficient, her two Hardy tender boats and rigid inflatable craft stored neatly on the foredeck, allow land visits from safe anchorages by way of lowering these craft by sling secured to a hydraulic crane into the waters below, thereby minimising the restrictions of berthing manoeuvres and departure deadlines.

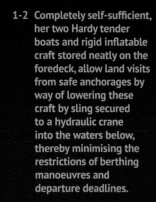

1

2

Hebridean Princess is no stranger to the waters of the Western Isles of Scotland having been built by Hall, Russell & Co., Aberdeen in 1964 as the *Columba*, one of a trio of car ferries constructed to an advanced specification for the Secretary of State for Scotland during the Cold War era. Immediately chartered back to and managed by her operator David MacBrayne, she operated services between Oban and Craignure and also Lochaline until replaced by larger car ferries at the end of the 1972 season.

Following two summers at Mallaig, she was redeployed at Oban in 1975 to replace the much-loved and elegant *King George V*, and offered cruises to Iona, Coll, Tiree and Colonsay, with additional calls at Lochaline and Tobermory. This was to be the start of her "cruising" history as she combined these island lifeline services with short mini-cruise combinations. She provided this type of cruising opportunity until her withdrawal from ferry service in 1988, after which her purchase by a family of Yorkshire canal boaters saw her transformed by George Prior Engineering, Great Yarmouth, into arguably todays smallest luxury cruise ship in the world – the legend of the "Hebridean Experience" had been born.

Re-named *Hebridean Princess* on 26th April, 1989 by Sarah Ferguson, the then Duchess of York, she began her new career with Hebridean on 26th May, conveying just 46 passengers around the Western Isles of Scotland in opulent luxury styled on a 5-star Country House Hotel at sea, and with a crew of 27.

Initially, passengers had an option to disembark their cars at certain ports within the itineraries other than Oban, but this concept was later refined giving way to additional cabins allowing for a substantial increase in the crew-to-guest ratio which by 1997 was the highest of any motor cruise ship in the world - 37 to 49. Now in her 25th season, and with the Hebridean Island Cruises philosophy that small is still beautiful still alive, she continues to cruise with a passenger complement of 50, each pampered in 30 magnificent staterooms, all individually styled in chintz or tartan and named after a West Coast Scottish island, castle, sound, loch or bay.

It is the "Hebridean Experience", from embarking at Oban to the skirl of a sole piper in full fig to the privacy and relaxation, gracious living, fine dining and personal onboard service where your smallest preference is remembered, which makes cruising with the "Small Cruise Ship Company" so exclusive.

On board is a sumptuous, intimate world where lavish furnishings and fittings speak of quality, refinement and a style reminiscent of a bygone era, set against a backdrop of staggering scenery and calls at remote colourful coastal villages, inaccessible to virtually anything but a private yacht.

A world of choice where "Footloose" cruises allow serious, energized trekkers to take scenic walks in the company of eclectic, fascinating passengers led by knowledgeable professional walking guides or strollers simply ambling the days away amongst the surrounding wildlife, and cruises offering the finest privately escorted tours to places of incredible natural beauty and local historic interest.

A world where night falls silent and remains hushed when the anchor is cast, often in remote, sheltered and tranquil bays, whilst the gloaming descends on a fiery Hebridean sunset over dinner. Like minded guests can exchange stories about the day's activities deep into the night in the delightful Tiree Lounge, complete with inglenook fireplace and as a retirement to a restful sleep is contemplated, the realities of the outside world will not only seem, but will be, far away.

Such features combine to create the Hebridean Island Cruises' trademark and reputation for excellence, inspiring guests to return time after time, ensuring that Hebridean Island Cruises remain the last word in luxury cruising.

Absorb the Clyde region's most treasured historic locations

around this beautiful and glorious landscape. Further north in Argyll, discover a land of mountains and lochs, of history and legend, of unsurpassed glory and lonely beaches.

THE CLYDE REGION, LOCH FYNE & AYRSHIRE

1

1   *Hebridean Princess* at anchor in Holy Loch, believed to have derived its name from 6th century when Saint Munn landed here from Ireland. It was used as a submarine base by the US Navy between 1961 and 1992.

2   The Gaelic equivalent of stone, Cloch Lighthouse was designed by Thomas Smith and his son-in-law Robert Stevenson and dates back to 1796. Built as one of three lighthouses to protect the waters at the head of the Firth of Clyde, the other two being on Little Cumbrae and at Toward Point on the Cowal peninsula, Cloch's role was to warn boats away from The Gantocks, a dangerous reef of drying rocks or skerry, directly west of the point. Its light was first shown on August 11th, 1797.

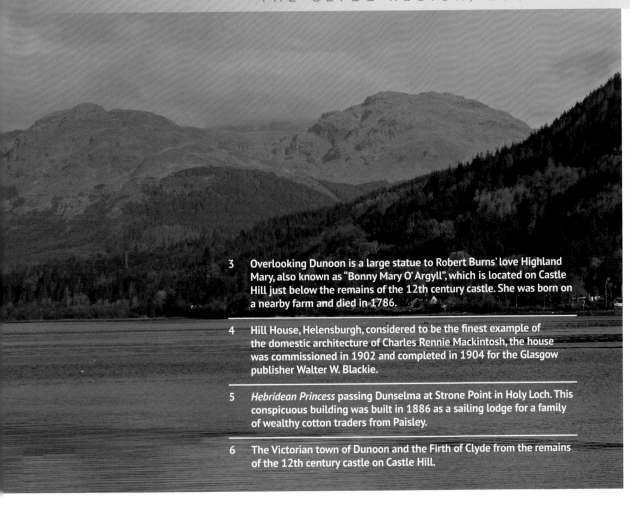

3   Overlooking Dunoon is a large statue to Robert Burns' love Highland Mary, also known as "Bonny Mary O' Argyll", which is located on Castle Hill just below the remains of the 12th century castle. She was born on a nearby farm and died in 1786.

4   Hill House, Helensburgh, considered to be the finest example of the domestic architecture of Charles Rennie Mackintosh, the house was commissioned in 1902 and completed in 1904 for the Glasgow publisher Walter W. Blackie.

5   *Hebridean Princess* passing Dunselma at Strone Point in Holy Loch. This conspicuous building was built in 1886 as a sailing lodge for a family of wealthy cotton traders from Paisley.

6   The Victorian town of Dunoon and the Firth of Clyde from the remains of the 12th century castle on Castle Hill.

1   The gaunt ruins of Carrick Castle stand on the west side of Loch Goil, dating mainly from the 15th century, though it was thought to stand on and earlier Norse site. Formerly a Campbell stronghold, the castle was burned in 1685.

2-3   The magnificently restored fernery at Benmore Botanic Garden was built at the height of this Victorian craze by James Duncan, a Greenock sugar refiner, when he acquired the 48-hectare Benmore Estate. Situated beside the dramatic mountainside of the Cowal peninsula, its magnificent gardens offer an enchanting walk through nature. Venture through a path of giant redwoods opening up to the formal garden and pond to overlook the panorama of the Clyde.

4   *Hebridean Princess* passing through the Kyle Narrows off Colintraive, which translates as "swimming narrows" – so named after the Bute graziers, who swam their cattle to and from the Argyllshire markets.

5   Turning in Loch Riddon, off Ormidale.

6-10 *Hebridean Princess* sails Loch Goil.

1 Originally built by the King of Norway in the 11th century to secure his conquest of the Western Isles, the great curtain walls of Rothesay Castle enclose a circular courtyard in the middle of the town, a feature unique in Scotland. Surrendered in the 13th century, it was lived in by King Robert II and Robert III. It also gave title to the first-created Scottish Dukedom, an honour held by the present Prince of Wales as his principal Scottish title.

2 The magnificent rhododendrons in the grounds of Mount Stuart House.

3 Mount Stuart House, Britain's most spectacular Victorian Gothic house and the architectural fantasy of 3rd Marquess of Bute, was designed by Sir Robert Rowland Anderson in the late 1870s.

4 At anchor in Millport Bay, Cumbrae.

5 At anchor in Rothesay Bay at sunrise on a beautiful autumnal morning.

6 Seating just 100 worshippers, the Cathedral of the Isles on Cumbrae Island is Europe's smallest but one of the most perfectly formed cathedrals. Designed by William Butterfield in 1849, this remarkable gem shrouded by trees at Millport Bay, was commissioned by George Boyle, later the 6th Earl of Glasgow.

1   Sunset at Largs viewed through the Viking longboat sculpture.

2   Regarded as one of Scotland's most beautiful natural woodlands, Kelburn Glen is also one of the most romantic, its network of pathways and footbridges dropping 700 feet by way of many waterfalls and deep gorges.

3   Ancestral home of the Earls of Glasgow since the creation of the title in 1703, Kelburn Castle was begun in the 13th and re-modified in the 16th century. Overlooking the Firth of Clyde, its appearance is more akin to a French chateau, the walls and turrets of the south side sporting a unique mural known as the Graffiti Project, created by four Brazillian Graffiti artists, and making Kelburn one of the most colourful castles in Scotland.

4   Kelburn Castle has a 13th century keep and splendid walled garden full of unusual shrubs peculiar to the west coast of Scotland, a New Zealand garden created by the Countess in 1898, a small formal garden designed by the 3rd Earl in the 1760's for his four children. The garden also contains two unique sundials, one of which can be seen here.

5   The round memorial tower on the shoreline just south of the town, stands to commemorate the decisive Battle of Largs in the autumn of 1263, where King Alexander III the last Celtic king, successfully countered an invasion by King Haakon of Norway's powerful fleet.

6   *Hebridean Princess* in Fairlie Roads with the snow covered mountains of Arran as a dramatic backdrop.

1   The Isle of Arran viewed from Fairlie with
    the *Hebridean Princess* berthed at the pier,
    the turn-around port used for Clyde-based
    cruises for a single season in 2009.

2-3 *Hebridean Princess* cruising Brodick Bay
    in the sparkling early season sunshine
    against the spectacular view of snow-
    covered Goat Fell with Brodick Castle on
    the foreground. Brodick Castle is located in
    the grounds of Britain's only island Country
    Park and offers 600 years of history, a
    fabulous collection of valuable artefacts,
    and stunning views over Brodick Bay to
    the Ayrshire Coast. Inside the Gardens are
    formal walled gardens and in excess of
    ten miles of marked trails. Brodick holds
    three national collections of rhododendron
    that flower in almost every month of the
    year. With its backdrop of mountain peaks,
    its terraced lawns and luxuriant gardens,
    Brodick Castle and Country Park is the
    epitome of a Victorian 'Highland' estate.

    This magnificent skyline is dominated
    by the snow-capped Goat Fell, which at
    2866 feet, is Arran's highest peak.

1   Inveraray.

2   Witness history at Inveraray Jail, bringing alive the conditions in a
     nineteenth century prison.

3,4 The 'Fairy Tale' castle of Inveraray, nestling beside the River Aray, is
     the home of the present Duke of Argyll. Designed by London architect
     Roger Morris, its construction for the third Duke who succeeded to
     the title in 1743, to replace the previous 15th century castle on the
     site, was supervised by William and John Adam. This unique piece of
     architecture incorporates Baroque, Palladian and Gothic styles, and
     has distinctive conical turrets, which give the building its chateau-like
     looks, and were only added after the castle suffered a fire in 1877. The
     Castle contains a fine collection of paintings, furniture, tapestries and
     Scottish weapons including the dirk, the traditional highland dagger,
     used by Rob Roy.

5-6 *Hebridean Princess* at anchor off Inveraray in November 2007, with
     the Arrochar Alps in the distance. This imposing town at the head of
     Loch Fyne was built in the second half of the 18th century, and still
     stands today in its original form. Loch Fyne measures almost 40 miles
     in length and was created by glaciers dispersing from the Southwest
     Grampians, which cut out the Lochs of Argyll. The dipping of the land
     allowed the sea lochs to be formed by the invasion of water. Inveraray,
     is regarded as one of the most attractive townscapes anywhere in
     Scotland.

1   A Grey Owl at the Scottish Owl Centre in
     Campbeltown.

2   *Hebridean Princess* cruising Loch Fyne, suffused
     in incandescent light following a passing
     shower.

3   The fishing boats in Tarbert harbour on Loch
     Fyne. Note the pine tree covered slopes of
     Loch Fyne in the distance. Not indigenous to
     the area, they came only in the 20th century
     as forestation schemes became bizarre tax-
     avoidance dodges for the wealthy and have
     changed the face of this landscape.

4, 5 Auchindrain Township, a unique and fascinating
     opportunity to see how a group of families
     lived, worked the land in common and played
     in the old Highlands. Consisting of an original
     set of farm buildings that have remained in situ
     surrounded by ancient field systems. Residents
     were self sufficient, growing oats, barley,
     potatoes and hay, rearing cattle and sheep, and
     with spinners, weavers, tailors, shoemakers
     and stonemasons working in support it was an
     early form of workers' co-operative. Agricultural
     improvements in the 18th and 19th centuries,
     the Highland Clearances and the development
     of crofting changed farming, families and the
     face of the Highlands forever, but Auchindrain
     remained virtually unaltered, just slowly
     evolving. The last resident moved away in 1967.

1   Royal Troon Golf Course is known worldwide for staging the Open Golf Championship and is the eternal haunt of history's greatest players. The Clubhouse was built in 1878 and designed by H.E. Clifford, the portico arched windows and cast iron balcony making it unique in Ayrshire. A spit of land extends from the resort into the Firth of Clyde.

2, 3   Ayrshire has close associations with the Scottish poet, Robert Burns, born in 1759 in a thatched cottage at Alloway. Built in the 1730's the cottage is by far the oldest house in the village and was an ale house for most of the 19th century until acquired by the Burns Monument Trust in 1880. It has since been immaculately restored and now houses the Robert Burns Birthplace Museum. Inside are many Burns relics, including his original writing set, manuscripts written in his own hand and the book that made him famous. The nearby Land O'Burns Centre commemorates his life and times.

4   Historic Dundonald Castle, perched on a spectacular hilltop location above the village, was built in 1371 for Robert II who became King of Scots, and was where he died in 1390. The grandson of Robert the Bruce, King Robert II was the first monarch of the House of Stewart and for the next 150 years Dundonald Castle served as a Royal residence for the Stewart Dynasty.

5   Romantic Culzean Castle, one of Scotland's greatest country houses and probably the finest Georgian castle in Scotland, was designed by Robert Adam in the 1770's for the tenth Earl of Cassillis, David Kennedy, on the site of an existing castle. Sitting proudly on one of Scotland's most spectacular clifftops the castle and the country park and gardens in which it stands, afford spectacular views across the Firth of Clyde to Arran and the Mull of Kintyre. Formerly the principal seat of the Kennedy family, the Marquess of Ailsa gave Culzean to the National Trust for Scotland in 1945, asking that part of the castle be given to General Eisenhower, for his lifetime as a thank you from Scotland for commanding Scottish soldiers in the Battle of Europe.

6   Experience over 250 years of living history at Dumfries House, built for William Crichton-Dalrymple, the 5th Earl of Dumfries between 1754 and 1759 and inherited in 1803 by John Stuart, Marquess of Bute. The House remains one of the Adam brothers' – and more importantly Robert Adam's – earliest architectural commissions. Its entire contents and a two thousand acre estate were dramatically saved from sale in 2007 by a consortium of charitable bodies led by HRH Prince Charles, Duke of Rothesay. Dumfries House has an unrivalled collection of Thomas Chippendale furniture from his early Director period, along with a significant range of pieces by contemporary Edinburgh cabinetmakers Alexander Peter, Francis Brodie and William Mathie.

The beach at Iona

Bay at the back of the ocean, Iona

1-2   Nestling on the western edge of the Crinan Canal, known in the 19th Century as "The Royal Route to the Highlands", is the tiny village of Crinan. With a population of less than 100, guests can wander the towpath by the side of the 15 simple, hand-powered locks and marvel at the feat of John Rennie's hand-dug Victorian engineering, which connects Loch Fyne with the Sound of Jura, saving the 130-mile sea passage around the Kintyre peninsula.

3   In the care of the National Trust for Scotland since 1992, Arduaine Gardens, are located on the Arduaine peninsula which separates Loch Melfort from Asknish Bay. Sheltered from the seashore by tall trees, the gardens are described as a plantsman's garden rather than a tourist attraction and are a place of peace and gentle charm.

4   Islay is famous for the peaty single malts produced by its eight distilleries, including the Caol Ila on the eastern side overlooking the Sound of Islay.

5   Castle Sween, under Norse control at the time of its construction, is arguably the earliest stone castle in Scotland dating from 1220AD.

6   Sunset over the romantic setting of Loch Craignish, with the yachting haven of Ardfern on the west shoreline.

7   Boat shed on the shores of
     the Sound of Islay.

8   Jura, meaning 'Deer Island'
     in Norse, is a wild, ruggedly
     scenic and remote island
     which is truly one of
     Britain's last wildernesses.
     A naturalists' paradise, it is
     roamed by 6,500 wild deer,
     outnumbering the human
     population by over 30 to 1.

9   *Hebridean Princess* cruising the Sound of Islay, a narrow stretch of water separating Islay
     and Jura. The 'Paps of Jura' can be seen rising majestically out of the sea in the distance.
     Their steep angles and shimmering quartzite shapes are amongst the most distinctive
     of all Scottish peaks.

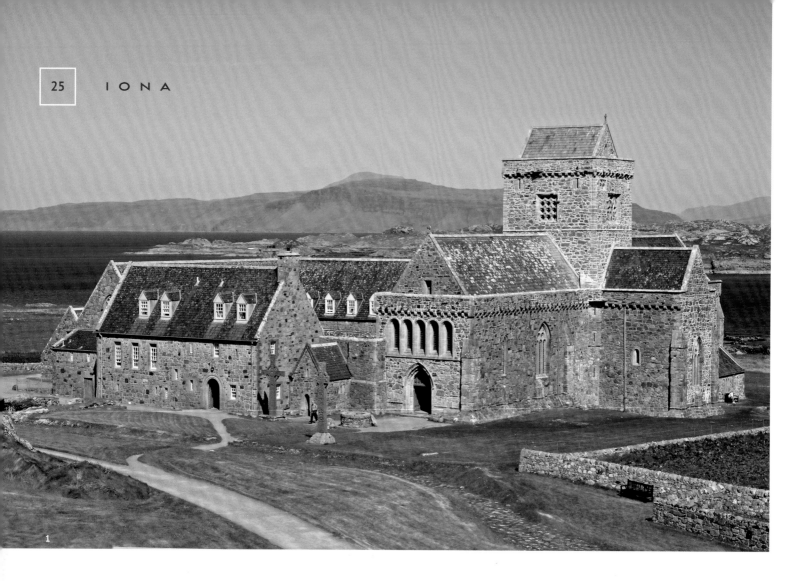

1. One of the oldest and most important religious centres in Western Europe, the restored Iona Abbey was a focal point for the spread of Christianity throughout Scotland and marks the foundation of a monastic community by St. Columba, when Iona was part of the Kingdom of *Dal Riata*. It remains today a much revered place of pilgrimage.

2. For centuries after, Iona became a place of pilgrimage and many great chieftains and 62 kings – forty eight Scottish, eight Norwegian, four Irish and two French - are said to be buried in St. Oran's Chapel and cemetery. Iona's most ancient structure, named after St. Columba's accomplice on his epic journey, it is believed to date from c.1080 and built on the instructions of Queen Margaret.

3. Standing 14 feet high and 18 inches broad, ornamented with sculptured figures, including the Holy family, David with the harp, and Daniel in the lion's den, St. Martin's Cross outside the abbey was erected in the memory of St. Martin of Tows who lived in the 6th century, but the cross probably dates from the 9th or 10th century. It is is one of the finest specimens of its kind in Scotland, its shaft decorated in the purest style of Celtic art.

4. One of the stunning beaches on the west coast of Iona.

5. Grey seals can frequently be seen basking in the sun off Iona.

6. *Hebridean Princess* at anchor in the Sound of Iona.

7. The Sound of Iona and the Dutchman's Cap.

1   Fingal's Cave on the now uninhabited amazing natural wonder of Staffa shows its immense and spectacular hexagonal, and in some areas pentagonal, basalt columns, formed from a molten lava flow 60 million years ago.

2   As the 1200 degree celsius liquid rock cooled, it hardened, shrank and fractured into a regular series of stone pillars. Although predominantly hexagonal, the cooling rate of the lava caused variations in the size and number of sides of these great basalt columns.

3   The basalt pillars which form the walkway around to Fingal's Cave.

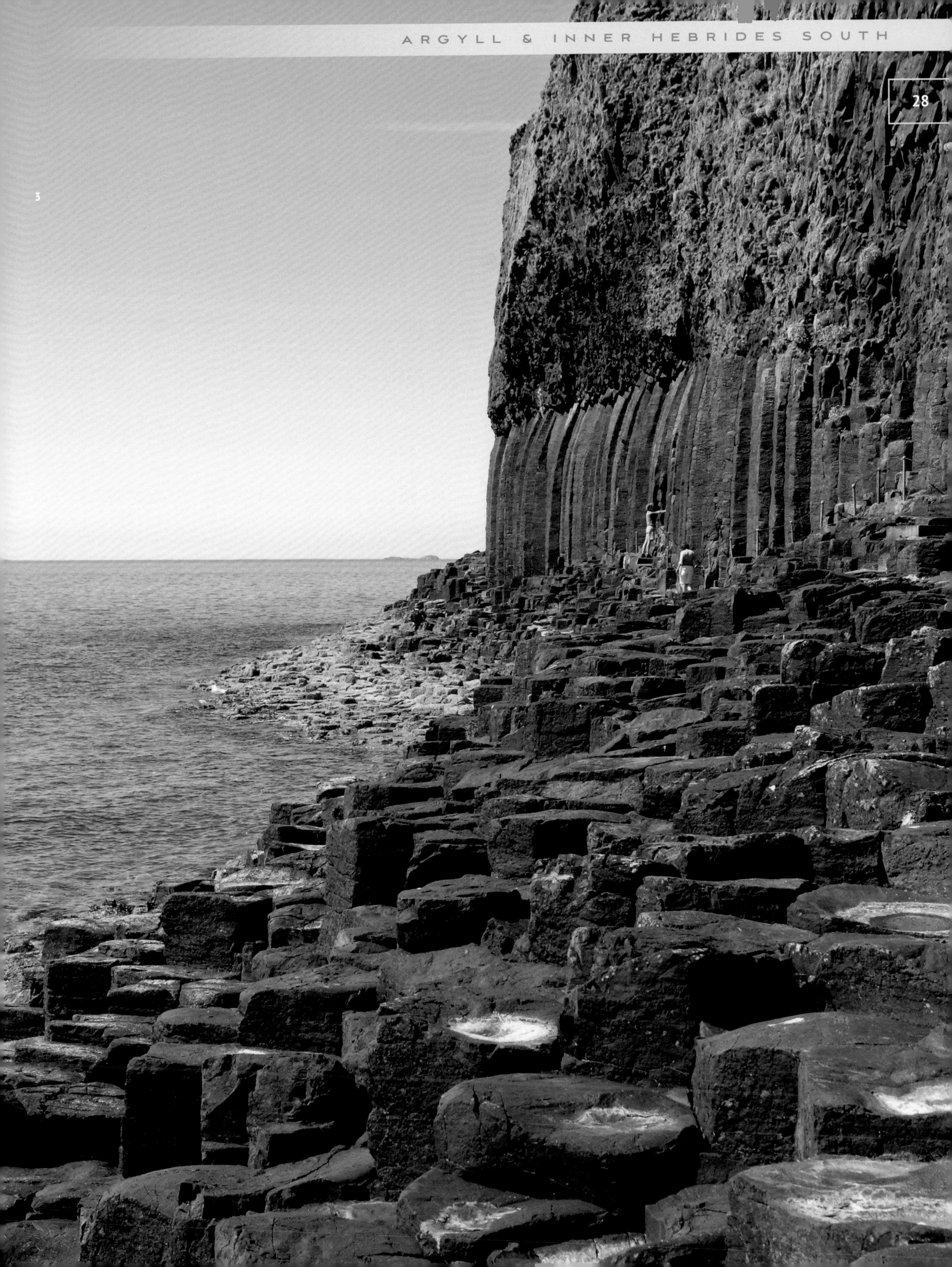

3

1   It is remarkable that this magnificent basaltic grotto remained undiscovered to the outer world until 1772 when visited by Sir Joseph Banks, who on his way to Ifceland was driven into the Sound of Mull, and there heard from the inhabitants of the great natural wonder. The cave takes its name, however, from the legendary Ossianic giant Finn McCool, who is credited with creating Staffa. The island, which has had no resident population since 1800, is owned and managed by the National Trust for Scotland, having been donated by the wealthy New Yorker John Elliot, who had initially purchased it for his wife.

2   Loch Tuath.

3-5 The tiny island of Ulva, home to Sheila's Cottage, a remarkably well restored traditional thatched croft house once the home of Sheila MacFadyen, a resident of the island who worked as a dairy maid for Ulva House and became too frail to manage life there. She moved to end her days on Mull in the 1950s, her cottage becoming a ruin. However, in the 1990s, the Howard family who own Ulva, undertook the restoration of the cottage, to house a museum and heritage centre for the island. The work, completed in 1998, was undertaken by skilled craftspeople from Mull, Skye and even Ireland. Learn about the famous visitors to Ulva, Boswell and Dr Johnson, Lachlan Macquarie and Sir Walter Scott. Beatrix Potter, a regular visitor to Ulva, found inspiration for many of her books here.

     The church on Ulva, built by Thomas Telford in 1828, indicating there was once a sizeable population on the island – it could accommodate approximately 300 for worship.

6-7 Coll is a rocky, wild island, first settled in the Stone Age. The near treeless island is scattered with ruined cottages, picturesquely clad in flower-scattered machair and fringed with silvery white beaches. It is a bird haven offering refreshing bike rides and walks.

8   Loch Na Keal.

1   *Hebridean Princess* cruising
    the Sound of Mull.

2   Thirteenth century Duart
    Castle, sitting on a prominent
    headland at the southern
    entrance to the Sound
    of Mull, has for over 700
    years been the ancestral
    home of the MacLean
    family. Originally built by
    the MacDougalls, it was
    in McLean hands by the
    fourteenth century, ruined
    by the Campbells in 1691,
    and was bought and restored
    by Colonel Sir Fitzroy
    MacLean in 1911.

1

3-6 Torosay Castle & Gardens - three formal Italianate terraces bloom colourfully with roses, other climbers and perennials, the path connecting the castle with the original walled garden lined by the most important collection of 18th century Venetian statues outside Italy.

1

1-2 Mishnish Lochs, from where the Tobermory Distillery sources its water. Mull's one and only distillery, and one of the oldest in Scotland was established in 1798 as the Ledaig Distillery.

3-4 Tobermory, from the Gaelic *Tobar-mhoire*, meaning the Well of Mary, is the colourful Capital of Mull with its 18th century Georgian facade. It was discovered by John Knox of the British Fisheries Society in 1786, who founded it as a fishing station two years later under the 5th Duke of Argyll.

Tobermory has two fine examples of rare Edward VIII red post boxes with oval sign retained above. Less than 100 of these rarities were cast before the short reign of King Edward VIII came to an end with his forced abdication in 1936.

5 *Hebridean Princess* in the peaceful seclusion of one of her overnight anchorages in Loch Na Lathaich off the coast of Mull. With all of its indented sea lochs, Mull's coastline extends to almost 300 miles in length. The great line of high cliffs in the distance are the North shores of Loch Scridain, rising some 1,200 feet from the Atlantic.

6 *Hebridean Princess* cruising the volcanic scenery around Mull, the most perfect being the "Dutchman's Cap", the southernmost of the Treshnish Isles, and just 284 feet high.

Sgurr nan Gillean and Sgurr am Bastein, Skye

Portree

Old Man of Storr, Skye

Rugged and weather-beaten,

the unspoilt spectacular landscapes and rich history of the Highlands has been shaped by a gigantic earth movement of cracking and slipping. Imbued with a soulful, wild beauty that is quite unique, remote Highland and Island Scotland is without doubt one of Europe's last wildernesses.

Quiraing

Raasay

THREE: INNER HEBRIDES NORTH

1 Known as the Jurassic coastline, the beaches and the Trotternish peninsula provide Scotland's finest fossil hunting territory.

2 Portree, *Port Righ* - 'Port of the King', named in commemoration of King James V's historic visit with his fleet of a dozen vessels to meet clan chieftains in 1540, it was also a port of departure during the notorious Clearances.

3 The Kilt Rock waterfall, tumbling over the precipitous cliff edge from nearby Loch Mealt in dramatic fashion and Kilt Rock itself, a striking vertical cliff-face of basalt formed some 57 million years ago, when volcanic molten rock forced its way upwards and then sideways through sedimentary rock lying on the seabed for over 100 million years. The top layer of Jurassic sandstone is today all but completely worn away, leaving the volcanic sills visible with a layer of sedimentary sandstone between them.

ROCK

1   Kilt Rock

2   *Hebridean Princess* creates a graceful arc in the waters off Kilt Rock.

3   One of the specially selected lunch
     venues on the themed "Gastronomic Tour
     of Skye" cruise, the Flodigarry Country
     House Hotel is situated adjacent to the
     cottage which was Flora MacDonald's
     last home from 1751 to 1759, and where
     five of her seven children were born.
     This sheltered haven, set in ancient
     woodlands in the small Gaelic township
     amongst some of the most dramatic
     scenery in the Scottish Highlands up on
     the Quiraing on Skye's Jurassic coastline,
     is steeped in the history and romance of
     the Jacobite past, which blend together
     to create something quite magical. The
     grounds of the hotel command fine views
     over Flodigarry Island, across the sea
     towards the Torridon mountain range
     and the broad sweep of Staffin Bay to
     mainland Scotland.

4   The Three Chimneys Restaurant, a
     converted 100-year old crofter's cottage
     located on the shores of Loch Dunvegan,
     has a long-established reputation for
     fine cuisine and also featured in the
     "Gastronomic Tour of Skye" cruise.

5-6 The Quiraing, one of the strangest and
     most fascinating mountains in Scotland,
     broken into ridges and pillars that
     resemble a mountain group in miniature
     rather than a single mountain.

1 *Hebridean Princess* approaching Dunvegan under the curious flat summits of the McLeod's Tables, their name dating from the 16th century when a MacLeod chief held an open air banquet for James V on one of them. Both are capped by a remnant of a tough lava sheet whose protection of the surrounding countryside has through aeons of geological time, been removed by ice and water, leaving the flat tops. The highest hills on the western moorlands of Skye in Duirinish, *Healabhal Bheag* reaches 1,601 feet, and *Healabhal Mhor* 1,538 feet. It seems incongruous that the lower of the two hills dominating this landscape is called *Mhor*, meaning 'big' and the higher is called *Bheag*, meaning 'little', although *Healabhal Mhor* is without doubt the bulkier of the two.

2 On top of a sheer cliff are the ruins of Duntulm Castle, an early 16th-century stronghold of the MacDonalds of Sleat. It was abandoned in 1730 after a nurse accidently dropped the laird's young son into the sea – his ghost is said to haunt the castle.

3-4 The Skye Museum of Island Life is a small museum consisting of seven traditional thatched crofters' cottages on the Trotternish peninsula. With superb views across to the Outer Hebrides, the cottages show the use of traditional building methods and materials that evolved over the centuries to suit local conditions and how life really was for crofters. Exhibits include memorabilia associated with Flora MacDonald and Bonnie Prince Charlie, the crofter's rebellions of the 19th century, clan warfare, and the history and prehistory of the region. The walls are up to three feet thick, with a steeply overhanging roof of thatch made from reeds or rushes. Included in the cottages on show here are a weaver's cottage, barn, smithy, and "Ceilidh House", where you can view a collection of old photographs and documents relating to island life.

5 Loch Dunvegan.

6 Dressed overall at anchor in Loch Dunvegan on the day of the Royal Wedding of HRH Prince William to Kate Middleton on 29th April, 2011.

7 The ancient seat of the MacLeods of Dunvegan and Harris, Dunvegan Castle dates from the early 1200's, going on record as the only residence in the United Kingdom to be continuously occupied by its owners. The oldest part of this much renovated site is the 14th century keep, with panoramic vistas across the Bay to the hills of Duirinish, MacLeod's Tables - *Healaval Bheag* and *Healaval Mhor* - the craggy Cuillin to the south and brown moorland to the east. MacLeod treasures include a 14th century silver mounted two litre drinking horn which traditionally all Chiefs must drain at one draught. Relics of 'Bonnie Prince Charlie' and manuscripts of Sir Walter Scott and Dr. Johnson are to be found here.

8 Dunvegan Castle Gardens.

9 A white Celtic cross in the churchyard at Kilmuir marks the burial place of Flora MacDonald in 1790.

1   Loch Harport and The Cuillin.

2   Craggy, grey, but majestic and totally out of keeping with the
     lushness of the region as a whole, Glen Brittle follows the east side
     of the narrow valley bottom, past the waterfall to its focal point
     at Glen Brittle House and farm. At the southern end of the Glen
     the River Brittle flows from its source in the Cuillin into the loch,
     fringed by a lovely beach. The area is a walker's paradise – and one
     of three routes into the awesome universe of the Skye Cuillin. The
     Minginish, the great promontory of which Glen Brittle forms part, is
     the wildest and least populated area of Skye.

3   The still waters at Struan on Skye.

4   Loch Harport.

5   Sailing into Uig Bay.

6   *Hebridean Princess* berthed alongside
    at Uig, backed by an arc of green hills.
    Fraser's folly tower can be seen in the
    foreground. Named after Capt. Fraser,
    the Laird of the day, the 1890-built
    tower was probably used by landlords to
    collect rent.

7   At anchor at Uig against the backdrop of
    Uig Bay and Loch Snizort.

1   Described as "Scotland's best known cook", Lady MacDonald shares secrets with guests in an entertaining cookery demonstration on the "Gastronomic Tour of Skye" cruise at the discreetly luxurious Kinloch Lodge Hotel. A truly unique place in a magical setting nestled at the foot of Kinloch Hill on the tranquil shoreline of the sea-loch *NaDal* in Sleat, the elegant drawing rooms provide a perfect setting for a Michelin-starred lunch.

2   *Hebridean Princess* off Armadale, with Ben Sgritheall, pronounced Skriol, towering 3,194 feet above Loch Hourn across the Sound of Sleat.

3   Loch Scavaig, where the black ridge of the Cuillin sweep down to the sea. Wander the sheer emptiness of the enclosed freshwater loch, Coruisk, one of only three in Scotland – the others being Loch Ness and Loch Awe. Pause to enjoy a truly mystical moment amongst huge rock slabs in the pure silence of this natural amphitheatre. Just two percent of the world's water is fresh water, much of it 'locked' inside rock and polar ice caps.

4   The ruins of Knock Castle, also known as *Caisteal Chamuis* (Castle Camus), lie on the east coast of the Sleat peninsula. Constructed by the Clan MacLeod and later captured by the Clan MacDonald in the late 15th century, ownership of the castle passed between the two clans several times before it was remodelled in 1596 by the MacDonalds. By 1689 the castle was abandoned and started to decay. Most of the stones were subsequently used to construct buildings in the area.

5   Passing Ornsay, one of the most beautiful tidal islands in Western Scotland. Situated to the east of the Sleat peninsula on Skye it provides good shelter to a natural harbour at Isleornsay, developed in the early 19th century as a herring port. It soon became a popular stopping-off point for the steamer from Glasgow. The "Ornsay" lighthouse was erected on the neighbouring islet, *Eilean Sionnach*, in 1857, automated in 1962 and modernised in 1988 when mains power was installed to replace the gas-powered system.

6-7   The Neo-Gothic ruin of Armadale Castle, the ancestral home of Clan Donald, dates from 1815 and is an extension to an earlier mansion house on the site from around 1790. A fire destroyed much of the house in the 1850's, and was replaced by the current central section designed by David Bryce. Abandoned by the MacDonald family in 1925, the castle fell into disrepair, but both the castle and 40-acre gardens are now home to the Clan Donald Centre, which operates the Museum of the Isles.

Glen Coe

Ballachulish

Ben Nevis

Oban

The "Gateway to the Isles"

and further north to Glencoe and the Highlands, this area is rich in ancient castles and tower houses, reflective of the feudal society which has shaped Scotland's turbulent history.

5

1   Gylen Castle, a clifftop ruin once called "the castle of fountains", enjoys a majestic setting on the south coast of the island. Built in 1582 beside a spring by the MacDougalls as their second stronghold, it was burnt to the ground by the Covenanter General Leslie in 1647. Its Oriel window situated over the main doorway entrance is unique in the surviving architecture of the West Highlands.

2   The grey clouds above Oban with pretty rainbow hues.

3   Looking across the Sound from Staffa Rock to Kerrera, once home to an important packing station for lobsters caught in Hebridean waters.

4-5 The hills behind Oban looking towards the Hebrides command fine views of Kerrera and Mull across the Firth of Lorn - one of the finest views in all Britain. Hutcheson's Monument, erected to commemorate David Hutcheson, one of the Victorian founders in 1835 of the steamer service from Oban to the Hebrides, is seen to the right of the picture.

      The delightful port of Oban is known as "The gateway to the Isles". Note the conspicuous Mc Caig's "Folly" Tower built at the beginning of the 20th century sitting on the hill behind this pretty little town. This iconic structure was constructed by a local banker of the same name as a job creation scheme for local unemployed stonemasons, but following the death of his wife, plans to house a museum and a 100-foot central tower failed to materialise and were abandoned.

1-2 *Hebridean Princess* off Dunstaffnage Castle in Ardmucknish Bay, with the mountains of Lismore and Morvern behind.

3-4 Oban harbour.

5 Close beside Dunstaffnage Castle is the outstanding Gothic chapel, with its ornate windows. In ruins, the chapel is still one of the loveliest gems of First Pointed Gothic in all Scotland.

6 The ruins of Dunstaffnage Castle, ancient capital of Picts preserving for centuries the 'Stone of Power' of Scone, now in the throne at Westminster Abbey, London. A ruin after a disastrous fire in the 19th century, the castle is surrounded by legends and tradition and by Clan wars and plotting. In 1746, Flora MacDonald, who helped Bonnie Prince Charlie escape to France after the defeat at Culloden, was arrested and held here briefly before being removed to the Tower of London.

7 Ardchatten Priory, founded in 1230 by Duncan MacDougall, Lord of the Isles, as a religious house of the Valliscaulian order and where in 1308, King Robert the Bruce assembled the last national council conducted in the Gaelic tongue. Burned by the MacDonalds in 1644, the principal portion now remaining was the Prior's lodge, now forming part of Ardchatten House. Its garden, with wonderful views extending over Loch Etive to Mull and Ben Cruachan, has existed here since its initial occupancy.

8 Oban harbour seen from McCaig's Folly.

1-3   The savage grandeur of Glencoe, its heather-clad steep slopes and dramatic jagged peaks witnessed the infamous massacre of the MacDonald clan in their own homes by their guests the Campbells in the early hours of 13th February, 1692. A dark moment in Scotland's history, the massacre came about when Highland clans were ordered to swear loyalty to King William III at Inveraray by 1st January, although many still supported the deposed James VII who had insisted on absolute power. Ian, chief of the MacDonalds failed to meet the deadline in time having mistakenly made for his old acquaintance Colonel Hill, Governor of the garrison at Inverlochy, who was not empowered to administer the oath, and although finally made some time later the Secretary of State John Dalrymple Master of Stair, rejected it and through government intervention ordered the massacre from Edinburgh. Troops then spent 12 days in the company of their unsuspecting hosts, enjoying their hospitality on the pretext that there was no room for them at their barracks. When the signal was given to carry out the massacre, some 38 were slaughtered and others died trying to escape through blizzard conditions in the vicinity.

The story is told at the Glencoe Visitor Centre.

4   Cruising Loch Linnhe.

6 The village of Corpach allows access to the western terminus of the spectacular 60-mile Caledonian Canal, designed to allow ships to avoid the double perils of the Pentland Firth and the marauding French privateers. One of Thomas Telford's masterpieces, construction of the canal was commenced in 1803 but only completed in 1847.

5 A classic fortified three-storey Scottish Tower House, Castle Stalker sits on its own rocky islet in Loch Linnhe. Thought to have been built by Duncan Stewart of Appin around 1540 for his kinsman James IV as a hunting lodge, the castle was garrisoned by Hanoverian troops during the Jacobite Rising of 1745 and after becoming roofless around 1840, is now restored to resemble the original building.

7 A heath-spotted orchid in Glencoe.

8 Neptune's Staircase, a series of eight locks lying between Corpach and Banavie on the Caledonian Canal, rises 72 feet in just 500 yards – the longest staircase lock in the UK.

9 *Hebridean Princess* passing through the Corran Narrows in Loch Linnhe with the wild hills of Ardgour behind. The route across this stretch of Loch Linnhe, just 218 yards at its narrowest point, lies on one of the ancient drove routes to Central Scotland and its cattle markets from the Hebrides.

10 Loch Linnhe.

1   The white sands at Morar on Scotland's stunning west coast.

2   The most remote public house in Britain, The Old Forge at Inverie, Loch Nevis. The village is home to a population of just 60 and still unconnected from Britain's road network. Accessible only by sea, it was the last community to survive the Highland Clearances.

3-4   Knoydart.

5   Landmark statue "Our Lady of Knoydart" stands guard over the entrance to Loch Nevis.

THE OLD FORGE

6 The Glenfinnan Monument, a round tower surmounted by the figure of a Highlander stands at the head of Loch Shiel at the spot where Prince Charles Edward Stuart raised his father's ill-fated royal standard to mark the beginning of the rising on 19th August, 1745.

1 *Hebridean Princess* approaching the Skye Bridge in Loch Alsh. The nearby village of Kyleakin was named after the Norwegian King Haakon IV, who is thought to have assembled his fleet of longships here before the Battle of Largs in 1263.

2-3 The Brochs of Glenelg, Dun Troddan and Dun Telve, are the best preserved on the mainland from pre-historic Britain. These drystone towers are amongst Scotland's most iconic archaeological monuments.

4   Eilean Donan Castle, set on a small islet at the meeting point of three lochs - Long, Duich and Alsh - with spectacular views of the western approaches to Skye. This forbidding stronghold of 13th century has long defensive associations dating back to the Picts.

5   The ruins of Castle Maol, erstwhile Dunakin – Haakon's Fort, which clings to a small island pinnacle just east of Kyleakin. Reputedly built by a Norse princess, upon her marriage to one of the MacKinnon chieftains, the site may date from as early as the 10th century. "Saucy Mary" as she was known, is said to have exacted the first tolls by extending a chain across the strait. After the Battle of Flodden in September 1513, Highland chieftains assembled here in an unsuccessful attempt to reinstate the Lords of the Isles.

6   The Kyle Rhea, or 'King's Strait', crossing the old Drover's road from the islands to the trysts of Crieff and Stirling. Upto 8,000 beasts were swum across here anually, tied nose to tail using heather or straw rope, until the arrival of the railway at Kyle in 1897. The cottage on the shoreline is the original Glenelg Inn, where Boswell and Johnson stayed during their Highland tour in 1773.

7   Departing Kyle of Lochalsh.

8   The 2,396-feet high *Beinn na Caillich* – "The Old Woman's Hill" in the distance.

1-2 *Hebridean Princess* in Loch Carron.

3   Duncraig Castle, built in 1866 in imposing Baronial style by Sir Alexander Matheson, who retired at the age of 36 after acquiring a fortune trading in the Far East through the Matheson Jardine Shipping Company.

4-7 The idyllic village of Plockton, situated in a sheltered cove by Loch Carron. Built at the beginning of the 19th century during the herring fishing boom, it is now an outstanding conservation area, and is preserved by building guidelines to allow future generations to appreciate its unique and historic setting. At its height the population grew to over 500, but after the herring deserted the shores and the 1846 potato famine struck, Plockton became known locally as the village of the poor.

8-9 Highland cattle grazing in Duirnish village.

10   A late evening scene in Loch Carron, brilliant flashes of sunlight silhouetting the *Hebridean Princess* as she approaches Plockton.

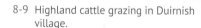

1   *Beinn Alligin*, formed mainly of Torridonian sandstone towers 3232ft above *Hebridean Princess* in Loch Shieldaig. The rock in the Torridon area is between 2600 and 3000 million years old, the oldest in Europe. Volcanic outpourings, massive climate changes, movement of the earth's crust, erosion, forestation, and finally the influence of mankind have all played their part in shaping this magnificent landscape.

2-4   In the centre of the loch sits Shieldaig Island, clothed in a thick mantle of fir trees, mainly Scots pine like the great Caledonian Forest which covered most of the Highlands many centuries ago. It was planted in the 1870's to supply the village with poles for ships and fishing nets. Designated a place of Special Scientific Interest, the isle now belongs to The National Trust for Scotland. Its thriving bird population includes herons, mergansers, black guillemots, kestrels and long-eared owls.

5 Cradled in the magnificent mountains of Wester Ross and lying on the wild shoreline of Loch Ewe, the world famous Inverewe Gardens were transformed by Osgood Mackenzie, stepson of the Laird of Gairloch in 1862, into an oasis of fertility on a Highland peninsula containing many rare and sub-tropical plants. Continued after his death in 1922 by his daughter Mrs. Mairi Sawyer, hydrangeas still flower in November, such is the effect of the North Atlantic Drift.

6-7 Stroll from Gairloch pier up to the Flowerdale Glen to the waterfalls in surroundings of complete peace and quiet.

8 The Torridon mountains.

1-3 The tranquil village of Applecross, where St. Maelrubha, a monk from the north of Ireland founded an early Celtic Christian community in 673AD, bringing the Christian faith to the native Picts. The monastery lasted until about 795AD, when it was destroyed by Viking raids. Of this establishment the only surviving relics are the cross-slab in the churchyard and further fragments with elaborate designs, inside the church. The present day building dates from 1817. The overgrown remains of a 15th century chapel on the site are barely visible in the churchyard.

4 Loch Kishorn viewed from the eastern aspect of The Bealach na Ba, or Pass of the Cattle, which was constructed in 1822, and is the highest and probably most spectacular pass in Scotland. Linking Loch Kishorn with the settlement of Applecross, this formidable road rises to 2053 feet in a little over 3 miles with gradients of almost one in three in places, making it one of the steepest access roads in Britain. Until 1975, when the mountain road was impassable in times of inclement weather, Applecross was accessible only by foot or by steamer service which ran between Stornoway and Kyle of Lochalsh, until the coast road from Shieldaig was completed.

5 Loch Carron.

A place of striking contrasts, the Outer Hebrides is both harsh and fertile, diverse and stunning. These wondrous isles have it all – white sandy beaches lapped by clear blue water, epic sea cliffs and stacks, heather moors and mountains hewn from some of the oldest rock on the planet.

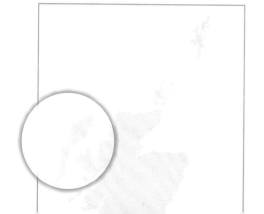

Kisimul Castle, Barra

Sunset in the Outer Hebrides

1 Castlebay, dominated by the remains of Kisimul Castle, standing isolated on a rocky islet in the heart of the bay. Once the stronghold of the MacNeil clan, those daring Hebridean pirates whose excesses not only troubled King James VI of Scotland, but also Queen Elizabeth, the castle is accessed by small boat from the village operated for Historic Scotland.

2 Barra Airport at Traigh Mhor with its natural cockle shell runway, has the only beach in the world to handle a scheduled air service, timings dictated by the twice daily low water.

3-4 Castlebay, formerly one of the principal herring-fishing ports on the west coast of Scotland, its herring industry story is told on the Herring Walks trail along the shoreline.

5 At anchor off Vatersay.

6-9 Barra: an extraordinarily barren island with over 1,000 species of wild flower and a beautiful little harbour at the capital, Castlebay.

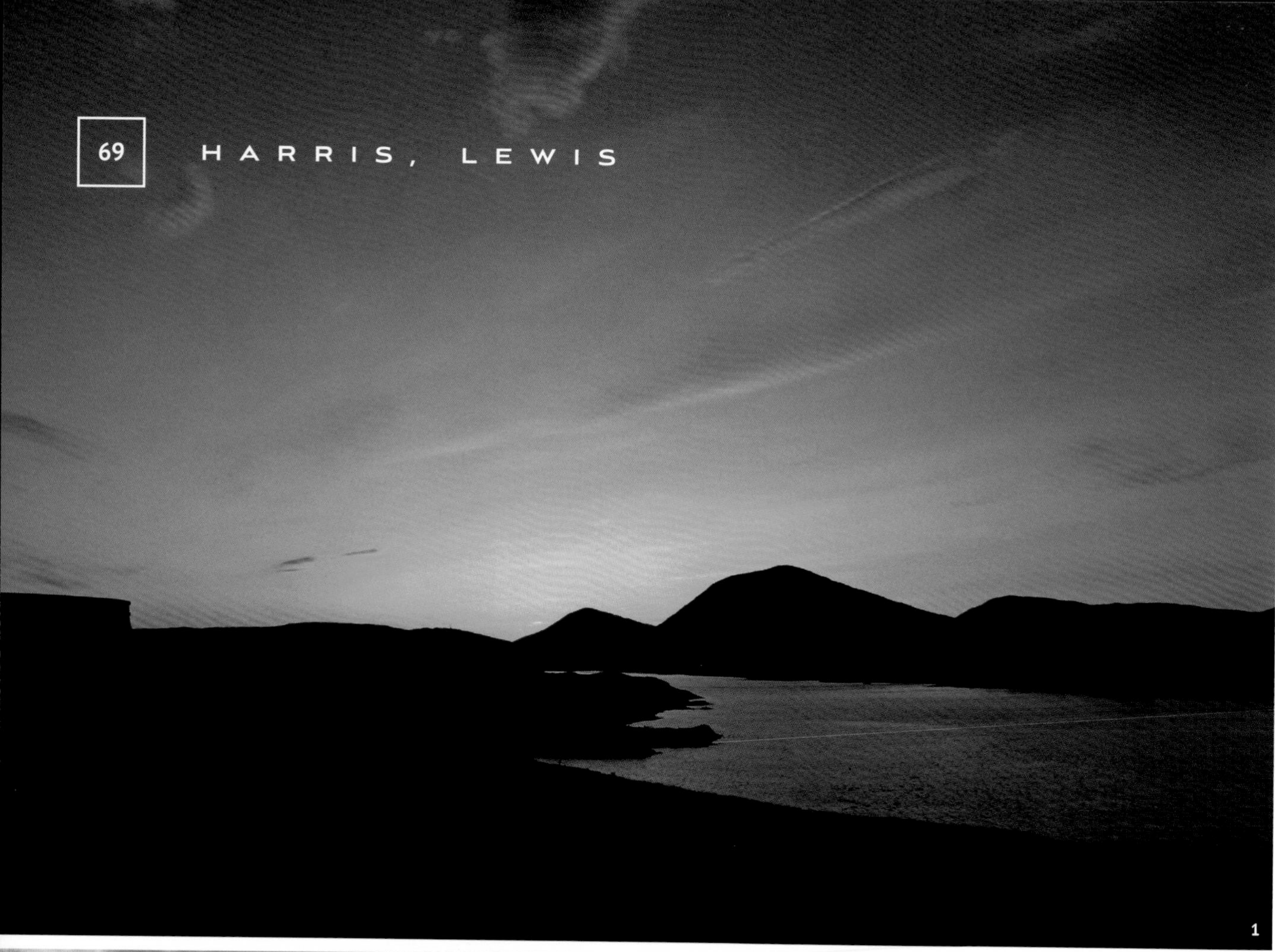

1

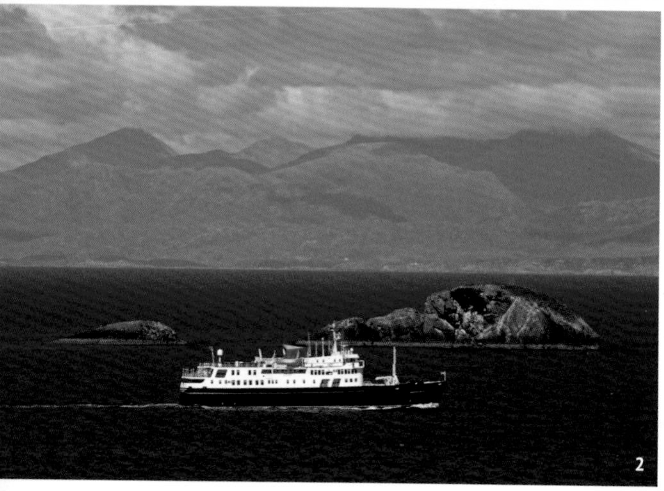

2

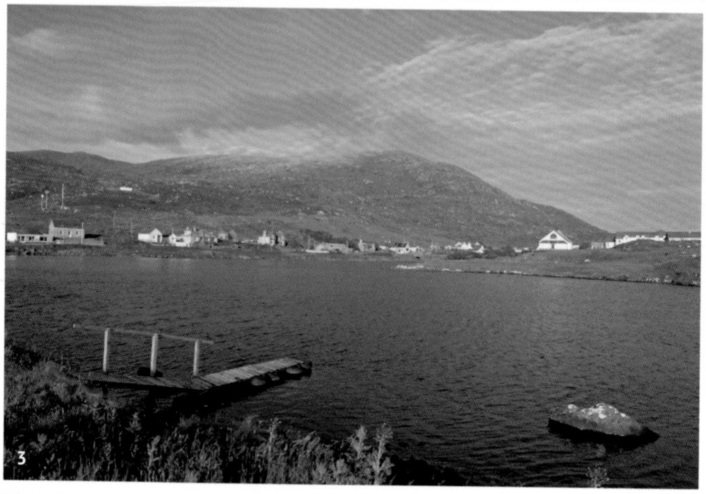

3

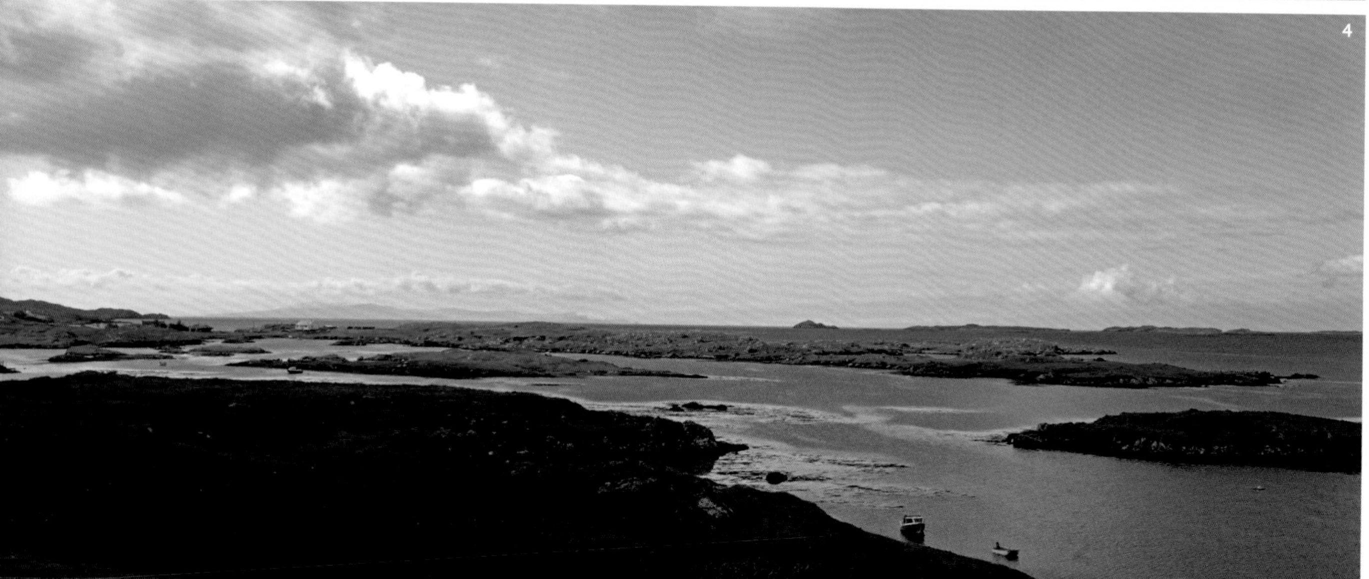

4

1-3   Harris.

4   The low lying islands to the south of Harris.

5   A basking shark seen below the waves in the Outer Hebrides, sieving the waters for plankton - look closely and you will pick out the gaping mouth.

6   Lews Castle, formerly the private residence of Lord Leverhulme but now in the hands of the Stornoway Trust, stands in the largest woodland of the Outer Hebrides. Here are over 250 spieces of tree, shrub, flowers, grasses and fern growing in James Matheson's original landscaping. Requisitioned by the Admiralty in World War II, the castle was used as a naval hospital, during which times the landscaped gardens of James McPherson deteriorated, but today this Category A-listed building is one of the most significant landmarks and focus of cultural and historic interest in Stornoway.

7-9   The entrance to the port of Lochmaddy, North Uist, is guarded by two 100-foot high craggy islets called the 'Maddies' (the "dogs" or "wolves").

1   Northern Gannets swarm high above Boreray, which at over 60,000 pairs on the islands and the surrounding stacs, constitutes the world's largest colony.

2   Village Bay from the lofty heights up to Conachair. The islands of St. Kilda rise out of the Atlantic Ocean 41 miles west of Benbecula in the Outer Hebrides, forming the last outpost of the north-west edge of Europe. People around the world have long held a special affection for these islands with their poignant history, dramatic scenery, spectacular seabirds and unique isolation. This incredible landscape provides a fascinating insight into the lifestyle of the islanders. St. Kilda is the UK's only listed mixed World Heritage site, renowned for both its outstanding natural and cultural heritage. There are just 29 sites in the world with this status.

3   *Stac Lee* (564ft) and *Stac an Armin* (643ft) off Boreray are the highest sea stacs in Britain.

4-5 At anchor in Village Bay, St. Kilda, where the Mark II QF gun sits on a promontory overlooking the bay in the foreground. This gun, which was never fired in anger, was erected after the island was shelled in May 1918 during World War I by a German U-Boat in response to a Royal Navy signal station linking the island to the mainland for the first time. Although there was no loss of life in the attack, the signal station was destroyed and the manse, church and jetty store damaged.

6   The crescent layout of a 19th century village remains to this day, along with over 1400 stone-built earth cells called cliets, for storing food - usually birds and eggs - by a process of salting and then wind-blowing.

7   A window on the world of the *Hebridean Princess* from one of the abandoned houses in what was the main street of Village Bay. The grazing Soay sheep also seen here are a unique survival of the most primitive breed in Europe dating back to the Bronze Age, and which are especially important for their genetic purity, ensured by their isolation.

8   The Feather Store, where fulmar and gannet feathers, bird oil and tweed were all kept and sold by the villagers in order to pay their rent.

The northernmost outposts of the British Isles,

these windswept yet alluring islands, with dramatic coastlines of soaring cliffs and white sandy shores set against clear blue waters, are warmed by the North Atlantic Drift. Steeped in history they boast a rich legacy of pre-historic sites as well as abundant birdlife in the many nature reserves.

The Old Man of Hoy, Orkney

Orkney

1   Berthed at Scrabster.

2   Located just six miles from mainland Scotland across the Pentland Firth, the Orkney archipelago consists of 70 isles and skerries, only 16 of which are inhabited. Dramatic coastlines of soaring cliffs and white sandy shores set against clear blue waters are warmed by the mild effects of the North Atlantic Drift and yet are closer to the Arctic Circle than to London. Not only known for its attractive scenery, Orkney is steeped in history and boasts an astounding legacy of over a thousand prehistoric sites - the best in Europe - earning UNESCO's recognition in 1999 under the World Heritage scheme, as well as abundant birdlife in its reserves and a wide variety of flora.

3-5 The Churchill Barriers: constructed between 1940 and 1945 on the orders of Winston Churchill during the Second World War following the sinking of the *HMS Royal Oak* by the German U-boat U47 on the night of 14th October 1939 with the loss of 833 lives, these four barriers totalled over three miles of causeway in length and linked the eastern islands. By 1943 over 1,700 men, including 1,200 Italian prisoners of war were engaged on the project, some of whom were also involved in the construction of the Italian Chapel on Lamb Holm.

The 930-ton, iron-masted motor schooner "*Reginald*" rests to the east of number 3 barrier in Weddell Sound, having been sunk in 1915 to prevent access to Scapa Flow and the British Navy from the East. Built in 1878 she is one of the oldest blockships and certainly one of the most complete. Today, she is used to store lobster creels.

6 Approaching Scrabster on a beautiful summer's evening with Dunnet Head, the furthest point north on the UK mainland, in the distance. One of the fiercest stretches of water in the world, the Pentland Firth is a narrow funnel of water between the Atlantic Ocean and the North Sea, where the rocky seabed and strong currents of the tidal flow can create confused seas and swells.

3 Stromness, which grew to importance as an 18th century trading post and final supply base on the Northern route across the Atlantic.

1 The 1141ft face of St. Johns Head is the tallest vertical sea cliff in the UK. Beyond, the 'Old Man of Hoy' stands off the Orkney island of Hoy itself, and can be viewed from the sea when crossing the Pentland Firth.

At 449-feet tall, this immense sandstone sea stack is Europe's tallest and the distance at which it now stands from the rock curtain of which it once formed part, is some indication of its antiquity. The 'Old Man' was first climbed over three days in 1966 by Chris Bonnington, Rusty Baillie and Tom Patey.

4 Kirkwall is dominated by the impressive red and yellow sandstone Cathedral of St Magnus, commissioned by Earl Rognvald-Kali Kolsson on behalf of his martyred uncle Magnus Erlendsson, killed on Egilsay c. 1116 on the orders of Earl Haakon Paulson. Work began in 1137 and took 300 years to complete. Part of the Cathedral known as 'The Choir' houses the tombs of both its founder and patron saint.

5 Originally 60 in number, the remaining 27 standing stones circle of the Ring of Brodgar, Temple of the Sun, set on a narrow exposed isthmus between freshwater Loch Harray and seawater Loch Stenness, about a mile north of the famous Standing Stones of Stenness, and is the northernmost example of circle henges in Britain. The site is believed to have been of special religious significance to the late Neolithic and early Bronze Age peoples and probably erected between 2500 to 2000 BC.

6-7 Begun on Lamb Holm in late 1943 and completed shortly before the end of World War Two, the delightful Italian Chapel was created from two corrugated Nissen huts by Italian prisoners of Camp 60 using mainly scrap materials. Restored to its former glory in 1960 by their leader, Signor Domenico Chiocchetti, who also crafted the sanctuary, it is an astounding tribute to their workmanship and dedication. The ornate interior with its altar rail cast in concrete is in stark contrast to its austere exterior.

8 Graemeshall World War II Coastal Defence Battery.

9 At North Haven in Fair Isle, a beautiful gem in the ocean just two miles wide. Occupied since the Bronze Age, it has many fascinating archaeological sites, including two from the Iron Age and is an important bird migration watch point, with a permanent bird observatory since 1948. (courtesy of David Wheeler).

With the spirit of Drake and Cook truly alive,

the great seafaring heritage of a nation is uncovered along the British Isles' East Coast and along the River Thames. Shipbuilding, first in wood, later in iron, was a major industry on the Thames from the medieval period up to 1911, when the last major shipyard, The Great Thames Ironworks and Shipbuilding Company at Bow Creek, closed after the London facilities found it increasingly difficult to compete with the lower cost shipyards of the Tyne and the Clyde.

1 Passing under the 8,300ft Victorian Forth Bridge, nominated in May 2011 for addition to the UNESCO World Heritage Sites in Scotland.

2 The bagpipes, seen as an instrument of war after the 1745 Jacobite uprising, were banned and went underground. It was only the continued use by the military bands of the Highland regiments which preserved this most iconic of Scottish instruments.

3-4 Under tow in Leith Harbour with the former Royal Yacht *Britannia*, decommissioned in 1997 after 968 official voyages and 44 years of service alongside at Ocean Terminal, now the centrepiece of a shopping and leisure complex.

5-6 Cruising the Firth of Forth, scene of the first air attack over Britain six weeks into World War II on 16th October, 1939. Despite being a prime target with the Naval Base at Rosyth nearby, the Forth Bridge has survived two world wars.

7 The more modern Forth Road Bridge was opened in 1964, the same year that *Hebridean Princess* was launched as *Columba*. A crossing of the Forth has existed here since the 11th century, when a ferry service was founded to transport religious pilgrims.

8 *Hebridean Princess* emerging from the docks at Hull in February 2009 following her winter refit. The light blue hull was retained solely for the 20th anniversary season.

1-3 Cruising into the River Tyne, where the north bank meets the sea, the ruins of Tynemouth Castle stand on the headland and enclose the remains of a Benedictine priory of 1090, where two saints were buried. Two walls of the presbytery still stand to their full height and can be seen here. A fortified gatehouse was added to the castle during the Border wars, which persuaded Henry VIII to retain the priory as a royal castle after the Dissolution.

4 On the River Tyne, the birthplace in 1907 of the liner *Mauretania*, which for 22 years held the record for the fastest Atlantic crossing.

5 St. Anne's Church in Newcastle, built in 1768 from designs by William Newton, is a Grade I listed building.

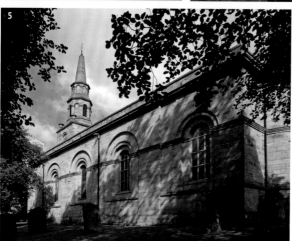

6-7 The 'New castle' from which the city derives its name was founded by Robert Curthose, son of William the Conqueror, in 1080. Originally built of wood and earth, it was rebuilt in stone between 1168 and 1178, work being interrupted in 1173 and 1174 as the castle was besieged by the Scots in consecutive years. The keep has survived as has the Black Gate, added between 1247 and 1250, and which was cut off from the keep by the construction of a railway line in 1847.

8

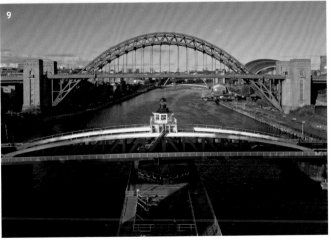

9

8 The striking Millennium Bridge, the latest of seven bridges spanning the River Tyne, was the world's first tilting bridge when opened in 2001 and has subsequently won more than 20 design and five lighting awards.

9 The Tyne Bridge, a prominent landmark in the city with its magnificent arch over the river, was built by Dorman Long of Middlesborough and was the largest single span bridge in Britain when it was opened by George V in 1928.

1   Entering the West India Dock, a spectacular end to her 20th anniversary season, to berth in the heart of the City of London beneath Canary Wharf. Here, City fund managers and analysts boarded for a series of promotional presentations to the Press and Travel Trade.

2   *Hebridean Princess* passing through the Thames barrier. Beyond is the O2 Arena, originally constructed as the Millennium Dome.

3-4   Cruising the Royal River Thames, a route well travelled by centuries of monarchs - all of the romance of this once-great port laid out on either side.

5   *HMS Belfast,* now a museum ship and permanently moored in the Upper Pool of the River Thames. This British-built Royal Navy Town-class light cruiser served during both WWII and the Korean War and in her day was one of the largest and most heavily armoured battleships afloat.

6   The Tower of London, erected by William the Conqueror. Traitors Gate is its most notorious entrance and leads to to the St. Thomas's Tower, where executions took place. Many notables have passed to meet their fate, including Anne Boleyn, Catherine Howard, and Lady Jane Grey. The last person to be judicially beheaded here was Lord Lovat, executed in 1747 for his part in the Jacobite rebellion. Flora Macdonald spent a year at the Tower of London for her part in allowing 'Bonnie Prince Charlie' to escape from Skye, before being released under the Act of Indemnity passed in 1747.

7   Berthed at Tilbury, Port of London Cruise Terminal. It was here where HM Queen Elizabeth II inspected the ship in November 2005 prior to the first Royal charter the following July on which Her Majesty enjoyed her 80th Birthday cruise.

8-9 *Hebridean Princess* at Tower Bridge, passing under the twin bascules of this once water-powered bridge.

10 The "Prospect of Whitby", dating from 1520, is one of London's oldest riverside public houses. Built during the expansion of the London Docks as a simple tavern, it gained a reputation by the 17th century as a meeting place for smugglers, pirates and villains, and became known as the 'Devil's Tavern'. After a fire in the 18th century it was rebuilt and renamed after a collier ship from Whitby in Yorkshire which moored nearby. Today there are barrels and ships masts built into the structure. Notable customers included Charles Dickens and Samuel Pepys. Behind the pub is Execution Dock, where pirates were once hanged.

10

8

9

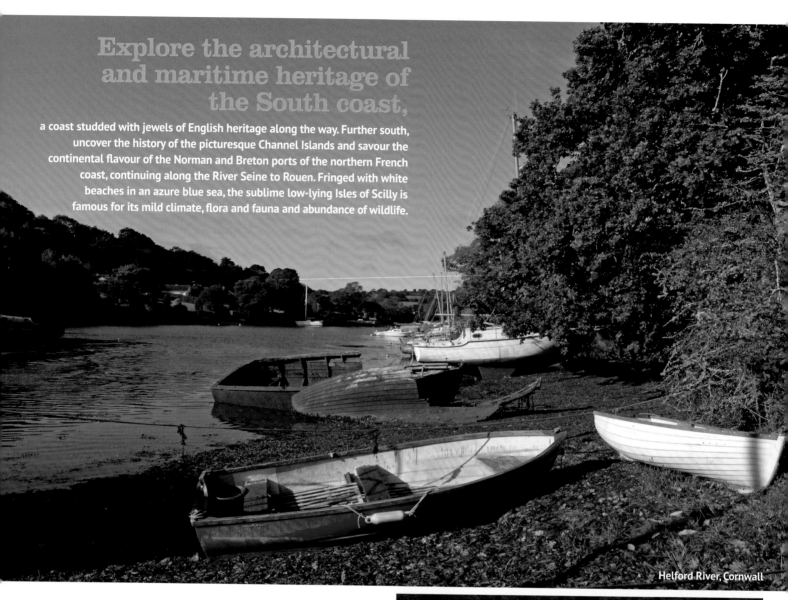

Explore the architectural and maritime heritage of the South coast,

a coast studded with jewels of English heritage along the way. Further south, uncover the history of the picturesque Channel Islands and savour the continental flavour of the Norman and Breton ports of the northern French coast, continuing along the River Seine to Rouen. Fringed with white beaches in an azure blue sea, the sublime low-lying Isles of Scilly is famous for its mild climate, flora and fauna and abundance of wildlife.

Helford River, Cornwall

River Seine

St. Peter Port, Guernsey

1-5   The enchanting 13th century double-moated Hever Castle, the childhood home of Queen Ann Boleyn, intriguing second wife of Henry VIII and mother of Queen Elizabeth I. Set in 30 acres of magnificent gardens, including an Italian garden with statuary and sculpture dating back 2000 years, the castle was restored and filled with treasures by William Waldorf Astor in 1903.

6-7   Lewes Castle looms high on a great mound above this attractive market town, which began its existence as a Saxon village and was the site of the Battle of Lewes in 1264 between Henry III and Simon de Montfort when their armies clashed outside the town walls, resulting in defeat for the king. Following the battle, de Montfort summoned England's first representative parliament.

8   Medieval Leeds Castle in Kent, stands on two small islands in the middle of a lake and surrounded by 500 acres of landscaped parkland and gardens. It dates back to the 9th century, was rebuilt in 1119 as a Norman fortress, and was later converted to a royal palace by Henry VIII.

9   The Royal Pavilion in Brighton, famous seaside pleasure palace of King George IV, is one of the most dazzling and exotic buildings in the British Isles. George, Prince of Wales, lived in it as Regent and as King and gathered about himself a brilliant and cultivated society. First built by Henry Holland in 1787 as a simple classical villa, the Royal Pavillion was rebuilt by John Nash between 1815 and 1822 in the Indian style. The interiors, on which George IV lavished enormous sums were decorated in the Chinese taste, which was carried to heights of splendour and magnificence never seen before.

10-11 Arriving at Dover with the impressive Norman Dover Castle standing on Castle Hill, the scene of military activity since the Iron Age to the present day, behind. The 'Key to England' as it is known, had its narrowest escape in 1216 when in a heroic siege it just managed to hold out against the French. There is much to see on the white cliffs including the secret underground wartime tunnels which provided a safe operations centre for the Dunkirk evacuations and the Battle of Britain, the Roman Lighthouse, now the bell tower of a fine Saxon church, and the great keep itself dating from 1181.

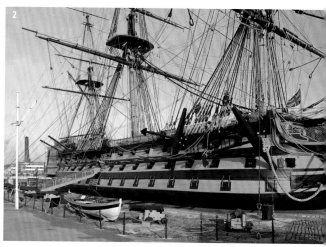

1   Old Portsmouth, also known as Spice Island after the area where Spices historically entered the city by sea. Royal permission had been granted in 1704 for houses to be built near to the dockyard and a new suburb called Portsmouth Common was created. This changed its name to Portsea in 1792 and soon outgrew the original town, which became known as Old Portsmouth.

2   Nelson's flagship, *HMS Victory*, famous for her role in the Battle of Trafalgar, along with a display of cannon.

3-6 For much of its long history, Portsmouth has been the home to the Royal Navy, which forged Britain's place in the world. Opposite *HMS Victory* stands the Royal Naval Museum, located in three magnificent Georgian storehouses built by local shipwrights. Originally founded in 1911 as the Dockyard Museum and refurbished in 1999, it displays a rich collection of artefacts – ship models, figureheads, swords, uniforms, medals and paintings, complementing four award winning exhibitions.

7   *HMS Warrior* of 1860, the world's first steam-powered iron-hulled armoured battle ship. When built she was the biggest, fastest and most heavily armed warship afloat and 127 years later made a triumphant return to Portsmouth as the last surviving example of the 'Black Battlefleet'. Now restored to her Victorian glory, a spectacular reception was held aboard this magnificent vessel during the 2009 'Jewels of English Heritage' cruise.

8-9 Osborne House was Queen Victoria's seaside residence overlooking the Solent, built by the famous London builder Thomas Cubitt at her own expense in 1845. The Prince Consort played a prominent part in the design of the house – it was his version of an Italian villa. The Queen spent much of her time here after Prince Albert's death in December 1861 and died herself here on 22nd January, 1901. The Royal apartments have been preserved more or less unaltered since.

10 *Hebridean Princess* moored in the narrow River Dart. Once a port trading in cloth and Bordeaux wines, the town is now home to the Britannia Royal Naval College seen here overlooking the estuary, and where the training of Royal naval officers has been continued since 1905.
(photo courtesy of Rodge Musselwhite)

1

1   It was from this man made beach at Trebah, for the D-Day Normandy landings practice routine, that 7,500 men from the 29th US infantry Division embarked on 1st June, 1944 to set off for their part in these historic events.

2-3   Trebah Gardens, its two-acre hydrangea valley casts clouds of china blue and soft white across Mallard Pond.

4   Sunset in Falmouth harbour.

5   *Hebridean Princess* passing St. Anthony's Head Lighthouse at the eastern entrance to Falmouth Harbour. Built in 1835, the lighthouse overlooks the spectacular entrance to the world's third largest natural harbour – The Carrick Roads and Fal Estuary. Its powerful 210,000 candle power light is fitted with a red sector that helps guide vessels clear of the infamous Manacles Rocks, eight miles to the south.

6   Built in 1545 on a high promontory, Pendennis Castle dominates the approach to the River Fal, and was part of Henry VIII's response to the Pope's threatened crusade against him, by fortifying his coastline. Together with St. Mawes Castle, Pendennis guarded the Fal Estuary, the latter seeing action in the Civil War, when "Jack-for-the-King" Arundell held the castle for five terrible months. Pendennis continued in military use until 1946.

7   The Roseland Peninsula - an Area of Outstanding Natural Beauty, characterised by sandy white beaches, defensive fortifications, and spectacular walks.

8-9   The National Maritime Museum Cornwall is situated amongst the cosmopolitan harbourside at Falmouth and houses the National Small Boat Collection.

4

7

5

8

6

9

1   At anchor off the Scilly Isles.

2-3 *Hebridean Princess* at sea. Known also as
     the Fortunate Isles, the Scilly Isles is a
     spectacular group of islands comprising
     of some 150 rocky isles off the coast
     of Cornwall. These gems, fringed by
     wonderful sandy beaches with spectacular
     views, are largely blissfully free from cars,
     crowds and pollution.

     Sailing through the Crow Sound on
     the safe passage to the north
     (photos courtesy of Christopher Hall).

4   The triangular rock formation of
     Hangman's Island, visible behind the ship's
     port quarter and situated between Bryher
     and Tresco, was thought to have been
     used as a gallows site during the Civil War.

5   Anchored off the island gem of Tresco,
     fringed with white beaches in an azure
     blue sea, it is famous for its Abbey
     Gardens, created in 1834 by Augustus
     Smith from tropical plants gathered by
     returning ships' masters.

6-9 Hugh Town, St. Marys, whose gardens are
     full of palm trees and birdsong.

4

6

5

7

8

9

1-2   Havelet Bay, St. Peter Port. Castle Cornet, Guernsey's ancient royal fortress, has stood guard over the town and harbour of St. Peter Port for almost eight centuries. It was the last Royalist stronghold to fall into Cromwell's hands during the Civil War in Britain in 1642.

3   The Victoria Tower in St. Peter Port commemorates the first visit to Guernsey of a reigning monarch on 24th August 1846, when Queen Victoria and Prince Albert paid a surprise visit to the island. Funded by public subscription, the tower cost £2,000.

4   The Red Drawing Room in Hauteville House, home to Victor Hugo, the famous exiled French novelist, dramatist and poet, draped with sumptuous pearl-encrusted embroidery. Almost all of the furniture and works of art have remained on the premises to this day.

Now preserved in its original state by the City of Paris, Hugo spent fifteen years in exile on the island between 1856-1870 for opposing the coup d'etat, staged by Napoleon III. Banished from Brussels and Jersey successively, he arrived in Guernsey and decorated the house, initially named Liberty House, entirely with his own interior design flair. He went on to write several of his masterpieces here, including *Toilers of the Sea* and *Les Miserables*.

5-8   St Peter Port.

9-12 *Hebridean Princess* at
      St Peter Port, Guernsey.

1-3 Noirmont Point on Jersey's south coast, where one of a trio of massive gruesome German Coastal Artillery Observation Towers was constructed. For Hitler, possession of the Channel Islands had been the first step in the invasion of mainland Britain, so in an attempt to make the islands impregnable nine were planned, but the remaining six were never built.

4 Berthed at the Albert Pier, Jersey

5 The South West tip of the island of Jersey is marked by the Corbiere Lighthouse, its name derived from the word Corbeau, French for crow, a bird traditionally taken to be an ill omen. Standing more than 100 feet above sea-level, it was built in 1874 and was the first in Britain to be built in concrete.

6 The impressive and iconic medieval Mont Orgueil Castle, a monumental part of Jersey's defensive history is poised on a rock above the small fishing village of Gorey. The presence of this mighty fortress is overpowering, completely dominating the harbourside at Gorey as it climbs up the sea-cliffs in a series of giant fortified terraces.

7 La Hougue Bie is Jersey's most noted archaeological site dating from around 3000BC. One of Europe's finest passage graves burrows 33-feet into a prehistoric artificial Neolithic mound, topped by the medieval chapel of Notre Dame de la Clarté forty feet above. The tunnel was aligned to allow the sun's rays to penetrate the inner chamber at Spring and Autumn equinoxes. The occupying forces in the Second World War constructed bunkers in and alongside the mound, which now form part of the museum.

8   The Jersey War Tunnels, where history runs deep, forcefully evokes the German Occupation of the island. Hohlgangsanlage 8 (Ho8) was constructed between 1941-1945 by forced and slave workers as an underground bombproof storage and repair facility. This vast tunnel complex was converted into a casualty receiving station, although never used as such.

9   The wide, sandy Royal Bay of Grouville, which gained its royal epithet after it impressed Queen Victoria during her visit in 1846.

10   The Monument to Freedom in Liberation Square, St. Helier.

11   The inspirational Jersey Tapestry, a work of art telling the story of the German Occupation and the everyday struggles of island folk during World War Two in vivid colour and intricate detail.

1-4 One of the prettiest of all French ports, Honfleur's Vieux Bassin was the birthplace of Boudin, who left 53 of his works to a museum which bears his name, and the workplace of other famous French impressionists such as Renoir, Cézanne and Pissarro.

5 The River Seine, France's longest inland navigation. Totalling 486 miles in length from the sea at Le Havre, it is navigable by ocean-going vessels only the 75 miles as far as Rouen. The tranquil green fields of the river valley, some of France's most mellow countryside of farmland and meadows, historic towns and sleepy picture postcard villages, such as Villequier and Duclair, adorn the riverside along its length.

6 Approaching the small attractive town of Duclair. The area around Duclair is famous for its orchards, its microclimate particularly suited to the production of different kinds of fruit including apples, pears and red fruits, all predominant on the banks of the river on the "Orchard Trail".

7 The Seine's infamous tidal bore known as *Le Mascaret,* was responsible for drowning Leopoldine, daughter of Victor Hugo and her husband Charles Vacquerie in 1843, just six months after their marriage. Dredging in 1965 mostly eliminated tidal bores on the river. *Hebridean Princess* is seen here cruising in the vicinity of this tragic accident.

1-2 *Hebridean Princess* disembarking the River Seine pilot off the medieval town of Caudebec-en-Caux, reconstructed in the form of an amphitheatre after severe fire damage during the Second World War in 1940. Eugene Boudin famously painted the town in 1889 as an outlet for his pain following the death of his wife.

3 Passing Le Mesnil on the "Orchard" trail, where apple orchards dot the route for several miles along the banks of the river.

4 A ferryboat crosses the Seine, making for a strange silhouette as the sun rises and the mist clears.

5

5   Passing under the 4,193ft cable-stayed Pont de Brotonne Bridge which, when completed in 1977, was the world's highest and steepest humpbacked bridge.

6   Hewn into the cliff face on the north bank of the river is a monument to five brave, near-forgotten aviators – Guilbaud, de Cuverville, Dietrichson, Brazy and Valette. In 1928, they flew to the Arctic Circle to rescue Italian balloonists who had crashed near Spitzbergen.

The Frenchmen were accompanied by the Norwegian explorer Amundsen and all were lost without trace in their Latham 47, built at the still-functioning aero factory nearby.

7   The haunted ruin of the Benedictine Jumieges Abbey with its 150-foot twin towers enclosing a Romanesque facade viewed from the banks of the Seine.

1   *Hebridean Princess* *de*parting her berth at Rouen with the Gustave Flaubert Bridge, named after the famous French writer of the infamous *Madame Bovary*.

2   Berthed at the cruise terminal at Rouen.

3   It took centuries to complete but Notre-Dame Cathedral in Rouen is a Gothic masterpiece with an intricately carved lacework on the stone facade and an imposing 495-feet high iron spire, the Lantern Tower, which when added in 1876 made it the tallest Cathedral in the world. Today it is still France's tallest cathedral and dominates the city's skyline. Immortalised by Claude Monet in a series of paintings, the interior of the cathedral is an object lesson in the history of stained glass through the ages, the wonderful rose-window over the west door being a masterpiece of 16th century art. Most of the present day Cathedral was built in the 13th century.

4   One of the principal Gothic monuments of Rouen, St. Ouen Roman Catholic Church is famous for both its architecture and its large Cavaille-Coll organ. Originally built as the abbey church of Saint Ouen for the Benedictine order, beginning in 1318 and interrupted by the Hundred Years' War, it was completed in the 15th century.

5   Medieval half timbered buildings and tiny alleyways in Rouen, one of France's most ancient and historic cities that survived World War II bomb damage. Known as the "City of 1000 Spires", Rouen was the scene of the trial and execution of Joan of Arc in 1431.

From the Western Isles to Ireland and the Isle of Man,

Velentia Island

embark on a trilogy of intriguing cultures – Gaelic, Celtic and Norse – through dramatic landscapes for the eternal spirit of the Gaels.

Peel Castle, Isle of Man

Giant's Causeway

1   Laxey Wheel or 'Lady Isabella' turns majestically in the peaceful Glen Mooar Valley as the largest working water wheel in the world at just over 72 feet in diameter, 227 feet circumference and 6 feet wide.

2-3   Maughold Village Church in the north of the Isle of Man. Saint Maughold landed on the headland in the 5th century and founded a monastery in the churchyard of the village, which still contains Celtic and Norse monuments, some dating back to 1000AD.

4   Castle Rushen at Castletown the islands ancient capital, is one of the best preserved medieval castles in Europe. With parts dating from 1153, it remained the joint seat of Government until the mid-17th century. Its towering limestone walls bear evidence of many sieges, including an attack by Robert the Bruce and are a continuous reminder to the local population of the dominance of the Kings and Lords of Mann.

5   Delightful Castletown harbour.

6

6   'The Calf Sound', a turbulent stretch of fast moving water
     separates the Calf of Man from the southern tip of the Isle
     of Man and is one of the most scenic locations in Britain.

7   Douglas, with its Victorian facade has been the capital
     of the Isle of Man since 1863. Settled since 6000BC, this
     small, independently spirited island, steeped in ancient
     Celtic traditions which stolidly survived the Vikings,
     boasts the oldest continuous parliament in the world,
     Tynwald, founded in AD 979. The island's highest point,
     Snaefell at 2036 feet, can be seen in the distance.

8-9 Cregneash village, a living museum housing a collection
     of thatched white-washed cottages, complete with
     Manx Loaghtan Sheep and a working farm, recreates
     daily life in a 19th century Manx crofting community.

10-11 Port Erin.

1   Rushen Abbey, the island's most important medieval religious site, built on land gifted to the monks of Furness in Cumbria by Viking King Olaf I in 1134.

2   Monks Bridge: A very rare example of a pack horse bridge in the British Isles. Built to facilitate the transit of the Silverburn River from the monks' farms in the north of the island c.1350 by the Monks of Rushen Abbey.

3   Peel's spectacular sunsets have earned it the reputation as the 'Sunset City'.

4   Tynwald Hill, from the Old Norse *thing vollr*, or 'assembly field'. Each year on July 5th, acts passed by the Manx parliament at Douglas are proclaimed on the tiered hillside by two judges or 'deemsters'. The ceremony, carried out in Manx and English, dates from at least AD 979.

5   The Old House of Keys in Castletown, former home to the Manx Parliament.

6-7   The Manx Nautical Museum at Castletown houses *Peggy*, a 1791-built armed yacht, now on the national Historic Ships register and one of the island's most precious treasures - in its original boathouse.

8   The Isle of Man Steam Railway was opened in 1874 and still operates with its original locomotives and carriages. The railway once covered over 50 miles but today only the southern section between Douglas and Port Erin survives.

9   Departing Peel, the only Manx city, by virtue of the ruins of the 13th century St. German's Cathedral within the grounds of the once venerable Peel Castle, seen here on St. Patricks Isle in the foreground. It was about 550AD that a Celtic type monastery was established on St Patrick's Isle, believed by monks who came from Ireland, and more than likely disciples of St Patrick. Thought to be the main residence of the Kings of Man until the 1200s and the historic seat of government on the island, it served in later years as a place for exiled state prisoners. Although used by the church due to the presence of the cathedral, when the roof collapsed in the 18th century, it was eventually abandoned.

10   Niarbyl is renowned for its spectacular views and is set in one of the most beautiful sections of coastline on the island. The beach here is one of the most important geological sites too, where rocks from two ancient continents were forced together 410 million years ago.

1

2

1   Berthed at Ballycastle.

2   At anchor off Bangor in Belfast Lough.

3-5 Ballycastle harbour. As the tide recedes in the late evening
     light, the stones on the beach are like enamel fresh from
     the furnace, bright and gleaming.

6   The rope bridge to Carrick-a-Rede island is 98ft deep and
     65ft wide and was erected by salmon fishermen to allow
     them access to Carrick-a-Reed island to check their nets.
     The geology, flora and fauna of the area has won Carrick-a-
     Rede recognition as an Area of Special Scientific Interest.

7   Bangor's North Pier, where mosaics depict
     the boroughs role in WWII, including
     General Dwight D. Eisenhower's historic
     send off to the hundreds of Allied ships
     gathered in Bangor Bay before the D-Day
     Liberation of Europe in 1945. It was
     renamed Eisenhower Pier in 2005 by his
     granddaughter.

8   A resort since Victorian times, Bangor
     now has the largest and most prestigious
     Marina in Northern Ireland boasting
     over 500 berths. Central pier is a unique
     opportunity to see at close quarters a
     rare colony of black guillemots nesting
     in the harbour wall. These are known
     affectionately as "Bangor Penguins".

1   The Antrim coastline.

2   Passing through the narrows separating the pretty port towns of Portaferry and Strangford in the unspoilt waters of Strangford Lough. Taken from the Norse words for "violent loch", the name reflects the passage of over 800 million gallons of water each day through these narrows. Extending over 80 square miles beyond are the peaceful and verdant shores of this perfect natural harbour, its entire shoreline a wildlife reserve and perfect for watching the many thousands of wading birds on the myriad of islands at its northern end.

3   Curlews are a distinctive feature of Strangford Lough, where they nest in winter. The Lough is one of three Northern Ireland estuaries holding numbers of national importance.
(photo courtesy of David Kennedy)

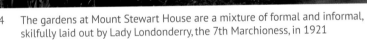

4   The gardens at Mount Stewart House are a mixture of formal and informal, skilfully laid out by Lady Londonderry, the 7th Marchioness, in 1921

5   Glenarm harbour.

6   White Park Sands on the stunning Antrim coastline.

7   Glenarm Castle, ancestral home to the Earls of Antrim for over 400 years, is at the heart of one of Northern Ireland's oldest estates. The Barbican Gate was built by Anne Catherine, Countess of Antrim, in 1825, having been designed by the Morrison brothers as part of her romantic redesign of the Castle and surrounding buildings. The Walled Garden is one of Ireland's oldest and was initially created to supply the Castle with its fruit and vegetables.

1-3 Passing through Dublin's East Link Bridge, her small size and shallow draught allowing *Hebridean Princess* to sail into the heart of the city to Sir John Rogerson Quay.

4 Trinity College library houses over three million volumes, including the treasured Book of Kells. This beautifully illustrated manuscript of the four gospels was written on vellum in the 9th century by monks from the island of Iona.

5 Designed by James Gandon and completed in 1791, the Custom House on the North bank of the River Liffey is one of Dublin's finest Georgian buildings. Set alight by Republicans in May 1921 in a blaze that burned for five days destroying many Irish records and reducing the building to a shell, the site has been wonderfully restored.

6 Wide Georgian doorways recall Dublin's heyday as one of Europe's foremost cities.

7 Dublin Castle's principal Georgian courtyard, flanked by the gates of fortitude and justice, corresponds closely to the castle enclosure established by King John of England and was the scene for the handover to the new Irish state in 1922.

8   At the foothills of the Wicklow Mountains lie the 49-acre gardens of Powerscourt House, long regarded as one of the most splendid in Europe.

9   Dublin's Ha'penny cast-iron pedestrian bridge spanning the city's river was built in 1816 to replace ferries, its name derived after a toll of a Ha'penny was applied to any person using it. The bridge itself was cast at Coalbrookdale in Shropshire and is used by some 27,000 pedestrians daily. It was closed between 2001 and 2003 for renovation work to be carried out by Harland and Wolff, the builders of *RMS Titanic*.

10   The famous Dublin landmark of the Four Courts, visible along the banks of the River Liffey, derives its name from the four traditional divisions of the Irish judicial system - the Chancery, King's Bench, Exchequer and Common Pleas. Seat of the High Court of Justice of Ireland, the site was occupied by anti-treaty men in 1922 and shelled by Irish Government troops, destroying the priceless archives of the adjoining Record Office relating to generations of Irish ancestors.

11   The peak of Slieve Foye towering over Louth's loveliest village, white-washed Carlingford, on the Cooley peninsula side of Carlingford Lough. King John's Castle, a 13th century fortress, dominant overlooking the harbour.

12   The *Hebridean Princess* on a peaceful summer's day in Carlingford Lough.

12

1   Early evening cruising the River Lee with Blackrock Castle and observatory on the water's edge. Constructed in the late 16th century to 'repel pirates and other invaders' from taking boats from the river, the castle was destroyed by fire in 1827 but rebuilt two years later with an additional three storeys. Today it is used as a centre for scientific research, outreach and communication for the younger generation.

2-5 Bustling Cork, or *Corcaig*, situated on wetland between two channels of the River Lee and unsurprisingly criss-crossed by bridges, it is Ireland's third largest city and means 'Marshy place'. It was founded by St. FinBarre in the 7th century as a monastic settlement. The courthouse, seen here on the north bank of the river dates from 1835 and was designed by James & GR Pain. Cork's superbly preserved 19th century prison (5) was closed down early in the 20th century.

6-7 Cobh: built on the site of the existing Parish Church of St. John the Baptist, the towering blue Dalkey granite cathedral of St. Colman's designed by Pugin, dates from 1868, its carillon of 42 bells greeting every cruise ship since 1916. A further five bells were added to this French Gothic structure in 1957 and a further two in 1998 for the great jubilee in AD2000, each tuned to the accuracy of a single vibration. Cobh has been the scene of many historic maritime moments – the *Sirius* departing for the first ever steam crossing of the Atlantic in 1838 and *Titanic* made her last call here on her ill-fated trip in April, 1912.

8 The impressive star-shaped Charles Fort of 1670 is one of the largest military forts in Ireland and has been associated with some of the most momentous events in Irish history, including the Williamite War in 1690 and the Irish Civil War of 1922. Its finely detailed and roofless 18th century barracks can be seen here within its colossal walls.

9-10 The now cosmopolitan 18th century town of Kinsale, a former naval station, is now considered to be the country's gourmet capital.

11-12 The quaint small fishing village of Schull, at the foot of Mount Gabriel, is a familiar landmark along the South coast of Ireland.

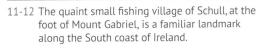

1-2 At the head of Bantry Bay, cradled idyllically between the dramatic Beara and Sheep's Head peninsulas, Bantry House is surrounded by gardens with wonderful views. This partly-Georgian mansion, ancestral seat of the White family, formerly Earls of Bantry since 1739, contains an impressive array of art treasures, including the Second Earl's collection of furniture and tapestries reputed to have belonged to Marie Antoinette. This small fishing village and market town survived two attacks by French troops allied with Irish nationalist leader Wolfe Tone in 1689 and 1796.

3 Beginish Island, Valentia, the European base for the transatlantic cable for almost 90 years until the mid 1960's. It was here that *HMS Agamemnon* landed the first successful transatlantic telegraph cable in August 1858, linking Knightstown to Hearts Content, Newfoundland.

4-6 The stunning scenery around Valentia.

7 The unusual prize-winning design of the Skellig Experience Interpretive Centre, where visitors are invited to discover more about the Skellig monks and the surrounding wildlife.

1-2 The erstwhile smugglers' haven of Castletownbere, where the legendary O'Sullivan Beare resisted the English at the Battle of Dunboy in 1602.

3-4 Cruising the Beara Peninsula, surreal from the sea, and onto Kerry and Valentia Island.

5 Departing Castletownbere with the assistance of the pilot.

6 *Hebridean Princess* at anchor off Garinish Island in the River Glengariff surrounded by wooded valleys and mountains. Ilnacullin Gardens were created in 1910 by the eminent English architect and garden designer Harold Peto for Annan Bryce, and are accessible to the general public only by privately licensed water buses or small ferry. This state-owned garden of rare beauty, bequeathed to the Irish people in 1953, contains a fine collection of trees, sub-tropical plants and bonsai, and with its appearance changing continuously with the seasons, it is considered Ireland's most outstanding.

7 Ilnacullin's beautiful Italianate gardens, pools and terraces were laid out between 1910 and 1913.

8 At anchor at Glengarriff against the Caha Mountain range.

Contrast the ultra-modern vibrant 21st century scenes

Caernarfon Castle

of the transformed industrial northwest with the serene, timeless appeal of romantic castles and charming old-world villages haunted by the ancient druids, dragons and dullahans of mysterious legend in Wales.

The Menai Strait

Manchester Ship Canal

Dinas Bran Castle, Llangollen

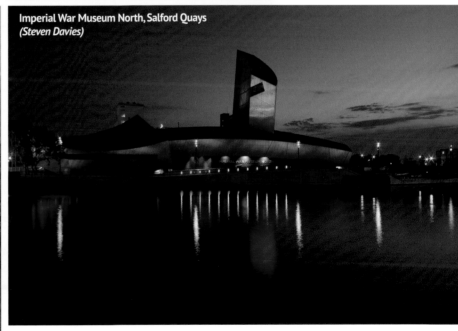
Imperial War Museum North, Salford Quays
(Steven Davies)

1   In the River Mersey, passing the famous Pier Head dominated by the twin towers of the 1911 Royal Liver Building, topped by the mythical Liver Birds. To the right is the 1916 Cunard Building and the green-domed Port of Liverpool building of 1907, a vestige from the city's past as a major port of passenger liners.

2   Passing Liverpool's Anglican Cathedral - Britain's largest - dating from 1904 but only entirely completed in 1978, en route for Eastham Locks to enter the Manchester Ship Canal. At 219 feet high and 31 tons, the bells of the Cathedral are the highest and heaviest in the world.

3   Construction of the 36-mile long Manchester Ship Canal eventually started on 11th November 1887 under Thomas Walker, when the first sod was cut from the earth at Eastham.

4   The industrial sprawl of Ellesmere Port and Stanlow Oil terminals.

5   Approaching Latchford Locks, Warrington.

6   When opened in 1961, the Widnes-Runcorn Silver Jubilee Bridge replaced the world's largest ever transporter bridge, and together with the railway bridge, this unique trio of cross-river bridges, never matched anywhere in the world, stood briefly until the demolition of the transporter later that year.

7   The powerful icon of two formerly operational cranes stand at Salford Quays as a reminder of the docks' heyday. Originally owned by Manchester Dry Docks Company which opened in 1894, the "Hurdy Gurdys" as they were known, were moved from Pomona Dock number 6 to their current site in 1988.

8   The original Manchester Ship Canal Dock Offices, opened in 1927, still stand amongst the modernity of Salford Quays.

9   The Manchester Ship Canal Company's Coat of Arms includes a steamship and a terrestrial globe reflecting the motto "Navigation and Commerce".

10   The wheels and chains of the lock gate's operating mechanism along the 36-mile Manchester Ship Canal.

11   The New Rising from the old: the most striking visible change of all is probably the transformation of the old grim docklands into the modern architectural miracle that is Salford Quays, around its jewel the Lowry Centre, the iridescent metallic and glass frame reflecting in the calm waters of the basin. Opened on 28th April 2000, the Lowry is dedicated to one of Salford's most famous sons, the artist Laurence Stephen Lowry (photo courtesy of Steven Davies).

12-13 The ancient Thelwall Ferry crossing between the village and the nature reserve at Thelwall Eyes, once rich farmland, is one of the last surviving one-man ferries in the country. So ancient and vital were the pathways and roads which the Ship Canal disrupted when booming Manchester drove it through between 1887 and 1894, legislation still demands it be operated by the Ship Canal Company.

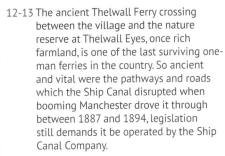

14   Journey's End at number 9 Dock, Salford Quays, initially built between 1899 and 1905 and opened by King Edward VII. A unique cruise through history along the Manchester Ship Canal, uncovering the industrial heritage of the North West along its banks, which are also home to a whole variety of birds and wildlife. Hebridean Princess remains the only dedicated cruise ship ever to transit the canal.

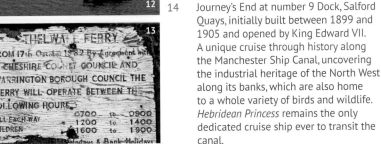

1   Silent guardian of the Menai Strait, Beaumaris Castle was the last and largest of the forbidding chain of Edward I's 'iron ring' of fortresses constructed as part of his plan to subdue the rebellious Welsh princes. Started in 1295 but never completed as the Welsh resistance fell away, it is widely acclaimed as one of the most outstanding military structures of its era and is a UNESCO World Heritage site.

2-3   *Hebridean Princess* passing under Menai Bridge, Thomas Telford's iron and limestone suspension bridge across the Menai Strait, which was the world's longest bridge of its kind, at 1266ft when it was opened in January 1826.

4   At anchor off Beaumaris with Puffin Island beyond.

6-7 Plas Newydd, Llangollen, combining romantic Gothic and Tudor style, it is extravagantly decorated with stained-glass windows and carved oak panelling. Here, Lady Eleanor Butler and Miss Sarah Ponsonby, known as the "Ladies of Llangollen" and immortalised by Sir Walter Scott in his delightful poem, entertained eminent guests including the Dukes of Wellington and Gloucester and William Wordsworth.

5 The picturesque and unusual Italianate village of Portmeirion lies in a secluded, almost Mediterranean setting and was the brainchild of Sir Bertram Clough William-Ellis, created between 1925 and 1976 to fulfil his lifelong passion for architecture. It was also the setting for the Cult 1960's TV drama series 'The Prisoner'.

8 Caernarfon Maritime Museum.

9 Plas Newydd on the shores of the Menai Straits, home of the Marquess of Anglesey, this ivy-clad house was altered extensively in the 18th century.

10 The weather-beaten ruins of Dinas Bran Castle, originally both a formidable medieval fortress and a splendid mansion for the Princes of Powys Fadog. The castle's short working life lasted scarcely two decades, from the early 1260's until it was deliberately destroyed to prevent its use by invaders during Edward I's initial Welsh campaign. In its heyday the castle featured a gatehouse, keep, hall, D-shaped tower and a large central courtyard and perhaps a chapel.

Serene and majestic, the Norwegian fjords,

spectacularly gouged out by the immense forces of ice sheets millions of years ago, lie at the last frontiers of Europe. They are amongst nature's greatest wonders and a source of energy for the mind.

Eidfjord

Bergen

Flam

1   *Hebridean Princess* alongside at Ulvik.

2   Cruising en route to the pretty village of Ulvik, with its orchards on the slopes. Norwegian folk dancing performed by local school children is a feature here during the evening stopover in the peaceful seclusion of the Ulvikfjord.

3-5   Eidfjord, known for its 350 burial mounds from the Iron Age and Viking periods.

6   The village of Herand, historic winner of the landscape prize at both provincial and national level and once rich from the boat-building which made it more prominent than Bergen, is now noted for the unique 150 or so Bronze Age rock carvings at the 9000 year old settlement in nearby Bakke. This fascinating collection includes many unique human forms, fertility symbols and ships, complete with hallows for sacrifices. Also in the village is the 19th century multi-bladed water driven gang saw, in regular use for boat-building until 1970. Listed in 1996 following restoration, it is the only one of its kind which has been driven commercially in Norway.

7   A Hardy tender alongside the small jetty at the tiny village of Sunndal.

8   At anchor off Aga in Sorfjord, a 25-mile arm of the Hardangerfjord. This little known gem is one of the few remaining group farms in Norway dating from the Middle Ages. The 30 remaining buildings, now listed, house an art exhibition, craft shops and special clothing collections.

10   Kinsarvik.

9   Utne, home to the Hardanger Folk Museum, which houses a fascinating collection of Norwegian artefacts, including many buildings preserving a way of life which has endured for centuries in this area. A traditional village settlement has been recreated in the outdoors museum. In the boathouses are many traditional Hardanger boats

1-3 Eidfjord, gateway to the 400ft Voringsvossen Waterfall.

4 At anchor in Sunndal, base for walking tour of the Bondhus glacier, an arm of Norway's third largest, Folgefonna. Covering 600 square kilometres, Folgefonna became Norway's 25th national park in 2005.

6 Herand.

7 Passing under the 750ft American-style road bridge built in 1937, which spans the width of Fyksesund, Norway's 'Secret Fjord'.

1-2 Ottenes, on the Aurlandsfjord between Aurland and Flam.

3-5 Aurlandsfjord.

6 Undredal, home to the smallest of Norway's 29 stave churches St. Nicholas Chapel, which dates from 1147 and has just 40 seats.

7 Seen at anchor from the elevated position at the head of Aurlandsfjord.

8

9

8 A close quarters view of the *Hebridean Princess* going alongside at Undredal in the blistering heat in 2008 during the 'Majesty of Norway' cruise. This quaint little fjord village of just 100 inhabitants was accessible only by boat until 1989.

9 Dusk in the Aurlandsfjord at Undredal

1   The Flam Railway, with 21 hand carved
     tunnels, took 20 years to build when
     completed in 1940. The 20-km journey
     ascends 2900 feet through lofty mountains,
     deep gorges, thundering waterfalls and
     peaceful green fertile meadows of the
     valley below, making it the steepest non-cog
     railway in the world.

2   Passing through Bakkasundet, the narrowest
     fjord in the world and shallowest stretch of
     the Naeroyfjord, at just 42ft deep and 820ft
     wide.

3   Berthed at Styvi: with no population for most of the year, this small protected farm village complete
     with collection of agricultural artefacts and exhibition of tools, is the starting point for the three mile
     footpath to Bleiklindi, part of the old postal route network which operated between Oslo and Bergen
     from 1647 to 1909. Steamers introduced in the 1860's, took over the service in 1876.

4   Gudvangen at the head of the Naeroyfjord, a branch of the Sognefjord, is often the scene of dramatic
     cloud formations around the many soaring peaks in the area. Waterfalls cascade down the side of
     towering mountains with peaks up to 4000 feet high, plunging into ice-scoured basins of between 980ft
     and 1640ft deep – a truly magnificent sight.

5   The stunning view of the UNESCO World Heritage listed Naeroy valley from the Stalheim Hotel,
     standing 886ft above sea-level. From Gudvangen one of Norway's and indeed Europe's steepest
     roads winds its way to the top of the canyon framed by two beautiful waterfalls, Stalheimsfossen and
     Sivlefossen, which cascade down the valley's side. The road up was built between 1842 and 1848 to
     improve the trans-mountain mail route and has seen few improvements since.

6

6   Under way off Balestrand.

1   Kvikne Hotel, with 210 rooms, has since 1877 been a landmark in the Sognefjord. One of the largest buildings in Northern Europe, this Swiss-style village has been a popular tourist destination for the British middle-classes since the mid 19th century.

2   St. Olav's Church, built in traditional dragon-style and known as the 'English Church', is part of the diocese of Gibraltar!

3-5 Scenes from around Balestrand.

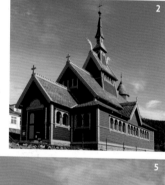

6-7 Vik, renowned for the only dairy in Norway still producing the traditional mature gamalost cheese.

8-9 Berthed at Laerdal, in its fashionable days once a favourite haunt of the 19th century English Salmon lords.

10 *Hebridean Princess* cruising the opaque emerald-green colour of the glacier meltwater of spectacular Fjaerlandsford. This magnificent colour results when minerals from the rocks eroded by the glacier enter the water of the fjord.

11 Sediment from the rocks carved out by moving ice sheets gives the glacier tongue a dirty back colour at its edges as it creeps down the mountainside at Fjaerland.

1

1-7 Geirangerfjord - this innermost arm of the
Storfjord stretches 15km and is deservedly
Norway's most popular fjord, cutting between
cliffs over 5000 feet high, and in places
almost as sheer. A myriad of waterfalls
cascade down the cliffs, notably the Bride's
Veil and the Seven Sisters (5).

8 *Hebridean Princess'* most Northerly cruise at
Alesund. Known well for the events of the
night of 22nd January, 1904, the wooden town
caught fire and as the winter winds fanned
the flames the town became an inferno,
leaving 12,000 residents homeless. The town
was completely re-built within three years
in the art-nouveau trend of the age after
help was sent by the last German Emperor
Kaiser Wilhelm II, and was the reason the
town alone, amongst the towns of More and
Romsdal, was not blitzed by the Nazis in the
Second World War.